K–12 CASE STUDIES
FOR SCHOOL ADMINISTRATORS

SOURCE BOOKS ON EDUCATION
VOLUME 52
GARLAND REFERENCE LIBRARY OF SOCIAL SCIENCE
VOLUME 1139

K–12 Case Studies for School Administrators
Problems, Issues, and Resources

Marcia M. Norton and Paula E. Lester

Garland Publishing, Inc.
A member of the Taylor & Francis Group
New York and London
1998

LB
2831
.82
.N47
1998

Library of Congress Cataloging-in-Publication Data

Norton, Marcia M.
    K–12 case studies for school administrators : problems, issues, and
resources / by Marcia M. Norton and Paula E. Lester.
        p.   cm. — (Garland reference library of social science ; v. 1139.
Source books on education ; v. 52)
    Includes bibliographical references and index.
    ISBN 0-8153-2570-3 (hc.)
    1. School administrators—United States—Case studies.   2. School
management and organization—United States—Case studies.   3. Educational leadership—United States—Case studies.   I. Norton, Marcia M.
II. Title.   III. Series: Garland reference library of social science ; v. 1139.
IV. Series: Garland reference library of social science. Source books on
education ; vol. 52.
LB2831.82.L47   1998
371.2'011'0973—dc21   98-16204
                                                                                    CIP

Printed on acid-free, 250-year-life paper
Manufactured in the United States of America

Contents

Introduction

Case studies enable aspiring administrators to refine their reaction skills as well as their critical-thinking skills by responding to a multitude of problems in a short time. Readers can assess their own administrative styles and attitudes as they respond to a variety of different situations, analyze their personal value systems within the cultural and political context of the organization, refine crucial interpersonal skills, and measure their beliefs against the expectations of the various constituencies with whom they must interact. The case studies in this book provide a broad-based overview of the kinds of real problems that schools are currently facing. The problems administrators face on a daily basis vary in scope and complexity. Professors of educational administration tend to avoid using case studies because they are reluctant to devote time in the classroom to lengthy case studies. However, students need exposure to multiple and varied real-life problem situations in order to develop their decision-making skills and leadership style as they prepare to become school administrators. Short cases provide opportunities to address, analyze, and resolve problems encountered in the real working environment. Students must actively engage in a process of inquiry and problem solving.

A school administrator's day is often a series of brief, disjointed, verbal encounters with different people seeking solutions or responses to a variety of situations. Administrators face demanding situations requiring quick decisions and a highly developed repertoire of critical-thinking skills. Administrators must be able to quickly shift mental and emotional gears and handle many problems and projects simultaneously. Administrative training should reflect these needs by exposing students to as many authentic problem-oriented situations as possible.

ORGANIZATION OF THIS BOOK

This book differs from other current case-study texts in that it presents brief cases that allow students to address many issues and problems within one course. Each case consists of a one- to two-page scenario that includes a statement of the problem in approximately two hundred words, followed by background information on the problem, and between three to five pertinent questions to be answered. The questions focus on the administrator's immediate response to the situation as well as the long-term consequences of this response. Cases give prospective administrators "dry runs" at situations they will encounter in their administrative career. It is possible to address up to three of these case studies in one class session, in addition to the regular lecture. Professors have the opportunity to cover their informational material as well as provide problem-based learning for the class. In addition, each case study contains up-to-date references that identify some published articles and documents available through ERIC (Educational Resources Information Center) that can provide additional insights into the issues in the cases.

ERIC is a bibliographic database (network of sixteen clearinghouses) that contains over 850,000 abstracts of documents and journal articles related to educational research and practice. It was established in 1966 and is updated quarterly in *Current Index to Journals in Education (CIJE)* and in *Resources in Education* (RIE). The use of an ED number (Clearinghouse Accession Number) in the reference list means that the document is not a journal article, but is one of the following other types of published and unpublished documents: research reports, curriculum and teaching guides, conference proceedings, project descriptions, and books. The following information is available when accessing an ERIC document through *RIE* or the Internet: abstract, accession number, author, availability, descriptors, identifiers, publication year, sponsoring agency, title, and pagination. A copy of the actual ERIC document is available at over nine hundred libraries that possess the ERIC microfiche collection, or the ERIC document can be ordered in either paper or microfiche from the ERIC Document Reproduction Service. If a document is not available from ERIC because of copyright restrictions, the abstract will provide information on where to acquire a copy of the document.

These case studies are about actual teachers. None of these cases are fictional, and the scope of the cases provides a broad-based perspective of administrative problems faced by principals and supervisors on a daily basis.

Chapter 1 of the book provides a history of the use of case studies. Chapter 2 describes different ways to use the case studies that would be helpful to professors and staff developers who may not be familiar with case-study methods. It discusses how to organize students into discussion groups; what parameters should be given to students; how to report on student reactions (debriefing); and how to look at various levels in each case (main problems as well as secondary problems, etc.). Chapter 3 contains case studies dealing with administrators, teachers, students, and parents at the elementary level. Chapter 4 contains case studies dealing with administrators, teachers, students, and parents at the middle-school and junior-high level. Chapter 5 contains case studies dealing with administrators, teachers, students, and parents at the high-school level. Chapter 6 contains case studies dealing with support staff at all levels. Case studies are arranged alphabetically according to topic within each chapter.

Finally, case studies are indexed by case numbers (1-140); personnel descriptors (bus driver, custodian, parent, student, teacher etc.); key descriptors (absenteeism, physical abuse, classroom management); and educational administration course (curriculum, personnel, school law, supervision, etc). In general, these cases may be used in urban, suburban, and rural settings as well as small, medium, and large school districts.

Readers can select cases based on their professional needs and interests, whether they are professors of educational administration; school-district staff developing in-service training for administrators; principal centers; or administrator and supervisor associations offering leadership training on the national, state, or regional level. This book can be used in several different administration courses depending on the case studies selected for class use. For example, it can be used in a general educational administration course, a personnel course, a supervision course, or a seminar in elementary and secondary administration. Finally, this book can be used over several years according to the case studies selected for class use. This is a multicourse, multiyear action case-study text.

This work was supported by the Dean of the School of Education and the C. W. Post Research Committee.

K–12 CASE STUDIES FOR SCHOOL ADMINISTRATORS

CHAPTER ONE

Historical Background of Case Studies

Case studies in various forms trace their origins to ancient Greece and China. Myths, for example, were allegorical narratives of episodes in the lives of legendary figures and served an important purpose by instructing the masses in the moral way of life. Apostles and theologians as well as teachers and philosophers used stories, parables, or narration of experiences to convey some "moral" or "teaching."

More recently, theorists such as John Dewey, Alfred North Whitehead, Jerome Bruner, Jean Piaget, and Benjamin Bloom contributed to the development of case method learning. The philosophical theories of John Dewey and Alfred North Whitehead provided the initial theoretical foundation. Dewey, the father of pragmatism, developed the concept that learning is rooted in experience and that knowledge derives from a process of inquiry that is often best found in the development of problem-solving situations (Dewey, 1938). Inherent in this concept is "active learning," which involves the learner as questioner and reflective participant. The learner becomes a "doer" and a "problem solver." It is generally agreed that this mode of learning is more effective and enduring than passive learning, in which the learner is the passive receiver of established knowledge.

In Whitehead's theory of intellectual progress, three states are described: "romance," "precision," and "generalization" (Whitehead, 1960). "Romance" introduces the student to active involvement with the learning situation, where an emotional connection and curiosity are present. Once active engagement takes place, the student moves to the "precision" stage, where he is required to systematically analyze and synthesize facts, data, generalizations, and concepts in order to understand the problems presented. The final stage, "generalization," integrates "romance" and "precision" and fosters intellectual satisfaction and a sense of closure.

Bruner's "theory of instruction" provides an additional influence. He emphasized the academic usefulness of games that involve people in the learning process (Bruner, 1975). Bruner discussed how problem-based learning activities place individuals initially in a state of "disequilibrium," which produces the need for explanation through questioning by the individual. These learning activities involve contrast, informed guessing, setting hypotheses, participation, and stimulation of self-consciousness.

Piaget was another contributor to the interactive situational approach. He theorized that knowledge and understanding develop when learners are actively involved in the learning process. In this theory, active involvement takes the form of problem solving and social interaction, producing qualitative changes in thought. Piaget's concepts of active involvement, autonomy, and constructivism are interrelated and emphasize experiential learning through which knowledge is not received from external sources but originates and evolves in the participants as they interact with and interpret environmental stimuli (Brainerd, 1978; Wadsworth, 1989).

Bloom's Taxonomy also has implications for case method application. Case studies are effective in the practice of Bloom's higher-level thinking skills of application, analysis, synthesis, and evaluation. They provide a way for the student to experience the interrelationship between course concepts and facts in real-life situations at the divergent, rather than the convergent, level of thinking skills.

Interest in the use of case studies as learning tools has been reported in the literature for the past one hundred years as a means of bridging the gap between academic knowledge and what happens in the "real world." As early as 1870, case studies were used at Harvard Law School. By 1915 the case method was the "pervasive methodology in the law schools of the country" (Culbertson, 1964), and in the 1930s case studies in public administration were developed (Asbaugh and Kasten, 1991).

In the 1940s case materials were developed for preparation programs for school administrators. The purpose of this early use of case studies was to provide "vicarious administrative experience and to afford the opportunities for intuitive decision-making" (Culbertson, 1964). It was not until the 1960s and 1970s, however, that colleges and universities began to use case studies to relate theories of educational administration to the practice in the field. The University Council for Educational Administration (UCEA) was at the forefront of case and simulation development during this era and published several "sets" of studies within the contextual, cultural framework of specific school districts. These case studies were developed in conjunction with administrators of actual school districts. During this period several case books were published for elementary and secondary school administrators. Authors included Hamburg (1957); Everett, Downing, and Leavitt (1967); Atkins, Bottom, et al. (1968); Ranniger, Bessent, and Greer (1969); Jarvis (1971); and Lloyd-Jones, Barry, and Wolf (1956) among others.

The impetus for developing and publishing case studies in the field of educational administration waned in the late 1970s and throughout the 1980s. Ironically, this decline in the use of practical reality-based case studies and simulations occurred at the same time that traditional preparation programs for educational administrators were coming under frequent attack.

There have been some common criticisms of administrative preparation programs including "the remoteness of academic programs from the problems of the field, the passive nature of most instruction, and the failure to present theoretical constructs in ways that are meaningful to students and practicing administrators" (Asbaugh and Kasten, 1991). In addition, graduates of educational administration programs complained (and continue to complain) that university programs did not provide the opportunity for applying theoretical knowledge to actual situations. These graduates also felt that the theory itself was often irrelevant to real-life situations.

Several other sources also criticized departments of educational administration for low standards, and failure to include "clinical experiences" as well as weak linkages to the practitioners and the real problems they face daily (Pitner1988; Achilles, 1984; Peterson and Finn 1985; Hawley, 1988; among others). Even more recently, in the first of two reports issued in 1991, the National Commission for the Principalship stated that graduate programs that prepare administrators for the public schools have failed to move with the times (*Chronicle of Higher Education*, January 9, 1991).

By 1985 the professional associations began to respond to this criticism. The National Association of Secondary School Principals (NASSP) published a special report titled *Performance-Based Preparation of Principals* (1985), which put forth recommendations for bridging the gap between the conceptual learning of the classroom and the requirements of professional practice. Recommendations included the use of case studies, simulation materials, computer simulations, instructional modules, group processes, and project courses. The National Commission on Excellence in Educational Administration's report in 1987 challenged scholars to seek new models for administrative training similar to those in professional medical, business, and law schools, which emphasize applied knowledge as well as theoretical and clinical knowledge. UCEA's Occasional Paper, *Educational Administration: Reform PDQ or RIP* suggested that "problems might well be posed through vehicles of computer simulations, cases, and filmed incidents, as well as actual problems in the schools" (Griffiths, 1988).

Reports that called for improving administrative preparation programs included two recommendations that focused on developing skills (analytical, problem solving, report writing) and using different instructional methods for content (case studies, simulations, role playing). The difference is between "knowing about" and "knowing how to do" certain tasks. Pitner (1988) recommended programs that more effectively mirror the actual working conditions of practicing administrators. He states that the principal's day involves "a continuous series of brief, disjointed, verbal encounters with a variety of people seeking solutions or responses to a multitude of contingencies." Principals face demanding situations requiring immediate decisions and a highly developed repertoire of critical-thinking skills. The job requires the principal to be able to quickly shift mental and emotional gears; therefore, administrative training should reflect these needs.

In the 1990s the focus in educational administration training programs has become broader based and addresses "problem-based learning." There is once again a growing interest in the use of case studies and simulations in administrative training programs, although it is not known whether these approaches have been widely adopted in educational administration classrooms.

In order to coordinate and consolidate efforts on a national level in developing problem-based learning activities, the National Policy

Board for Educational Administration and the Danforth Foundation sponsored a national conference on "Problem Based Learning for Educational Leadership Programs" in San Francisco in April 1992. This conference was the first national meeting of educators interested in developing a problem-based approach to preparing school leaders. The program featured general sessions on the theory and practice of problem-based instruction and fourteen extended, "hands-on" workshops that allowed the participants to experience the problem-based approach. The National Policy Board for Educational Administration has subsequently identified 21 administrative skill areas within 4 domains (functional, programmatic, interpersonal, and contextual). Leadership Training Associates and The National Association of Secondary Principals have developed training modules in several of the domains that contain case study materials for practicing administrators.

Problem-based learning using the case-study approach can help alleviate current training deficits. This approach provides opportunities for participants to assess their own administrative styles and attitudes, to analyze their personal value systems within the cultural and political context of the organization, and to measure their beliefs against the expectations of the various constituencies with whom they must interact. The case-study method also provides opportunities to address, analyze, and resolve problems encountered in the real working environment. In order to solve the problems with which they are confronted, students have to engage in a process of inquiry and problem analysis in an active manner.

Case studies can be responsive to particular contexts and are ideal for training in a time of reform and restructuring in public education. The context of schooling has changed and continues to change. In addition, social and institutional changes are constantly taking place. Carefully developed case studies can capture this context in a way that enhances the training of new school leaders as well as the retraining of present school leaders.

The case-method approach provides a safe environment and time for reflection, analysis, and feedback. Case studies afford the aspiring administrator an opportunity to address problems in near-real situations in preservice programs. They also provide practicing administrators with the opportunity to expand their repertoire of administrative skills through in-service programs. The case-study approach can provide students of educational administration with the needed grounding in appraisal of specific situations and the opportunity to discover alternative interpretations and choices of strategies as they refine their decision-making and communication skills.

There seems to be a general agreement that cases and simulations provide a means for in-depth analysis, which supplements technical skills covered in text and lecture material and that these, and other problem-based learning approaches, are essential components of future training programs for school administrators. Case studies alleviate the problems that new administrators encounter when they attempt to integrate what they have learned in class and from texts and have difficulty accomplishing this because of the complexity and uncertainty of the problems, and the intangible nature of human interactions in any given situation. Transfer of training is facilitated when the students see the connection between what they have learned and the present situation confronting them. Case studies allow the students to apply theoretical analysis because they are removed from the pressures and sense of urgency of the school setting.

REFERENCES

Achilles, C. 1984. Forecast: Stormy Weather Ahead in Educational Administration. *Issues in Education II(2).*

Asbaugh, C.R., and K. Kasten. 1991. *Educational Leadership: Case Studies for Reflective Practice.* White Plains, NY. Longman Publishing Group.

Atkins, T., and R. Bottom et al. 1968. *Simulated Case Studies.* Washington, DC. Department of Elementary School Principals.

Brainerd, C.J. 1978. *Piaget's Theory of Intelligence.* Englewood Cliffs, NJ. Prentice-Hall.

Bruner, J. 1975. *Towards a Theory of Instruction.* Bellnap Press.

Chronicle of Higher Education. January 9, 1991. Teacher Education Update.

Culbertson, J. 1964. The Preparation of Administrators. In D.E. Griffiths,ed. *Behavioral Science and Educational Administration.* The 63rd Yearbook of the National Society for the Study of Education. Chicago, IL. National Society for the Study of Education (NSSE).

Dewey, J. 1938. *Experience and Education.* New York, NY. Macmillan.

Everett, J.B., M. Downing, and H. Leavitt. 1967. *Case Studies in School Supervision.* New York, NY. Holt, Rinehart and Winston.

Gorton, R. 1987. *School Leadership and Administration,* 3rd edition. Dubuque, Iowa. Wm. C. Brown Company, Publishers.

Griffiths, D. 1988. *Educational Administration: Reform PDQ or RIP*. Tempe, AZ. The University Council for Educational Administration.

Griffiths, D., R. Stout, and P. Forsyth 1988. *Leaders for America's Schools*. Berkeley, CA. McCutchan Publishing Corporation.

Hamburg, Morris. 1957. *Case Studies in Elementary School Administration*. New York, NY. Teachers College Press.

Hawley, W.D. 1988. Universities and the Improvement of School Management: Role for the States. In *Leaders for America's Schools*. Berkeley, CA. McCutchan Publishing Corporation.

Hutchings, P. 1993. *Using Cases to Improve College Teaching: A Guide to Reflective Practice*. Washington, DC. American Association for Higher Education.

Kirschman, R. 1996. *Educational Administration: A Collection of Case Studies*. Englewood Cliffs, NJ. Prentice-Hall.

Kowalski, T. 1991. *Case Studies in Educational Administration*. White Plains, NY. Longman Publishing Group.

Lloyd-Jones, E., R. Barry, and B. Wolf. 1956. *Case Studies in Human Relationships in Secondary School*. New York, NY. Teachers College Press.

Jarvis, O.T. 1971. *Cases in Elementary School Administration*. Dubuque, IO. Wm. C. Brown Company, Publishers.

Performance-Based Preparation of Principals. 1985. Reston, VA. National Association of Secondary School Principals.

Peterson, K, and C. Finn. 1985. Principals, Superintendents, and the Administrator's Art. *The Public Interest, 79*.

Pitner, N. 1988. Training of the School Administrator: State of the Art In *Leaders for America's Schools*. Berkeley, CA. McCutchan Publishing Corporation.

Ranniger, B., J. Bessent and J.T. Greer. 1969. *Elementary School Administration: A Casebook*. Scranton, PA. International Textbook Company.

Shulman, J.H., ed. 1992. *Case Methods in Teacher Education*. New York, NY. Teachers College Press.

Wadsworth, B.J. 1989. *Piaget's Theory of Cognitive and Affective Development*. White Plains, NY. Longman Publishing Group.

Wasserman, S. 1993. *Getting Down to Cases: Learning to Teach with Case Studies*. New York, NY. Teachers College Press.

Wasserman, S. 1994. *Introduction to Case Method Teaching: A Guide to the Galaxy*. New York, NY. Teachers College Press.

Whitehead, A.N. 1960. *Process and Reality*. New York, NY. Harper and Row.

Yin, R.K. 1984. *Case Study Research: Design and Methods.* Beverly Hills, CA. SAGE Publications, Inc.

Zuelke, S. and M. Willerman. 1991. *Vignettes and Cases in Elementary Administration.* Dubuque, Iowa. Wm. C. Brown Company, Publishers.

CHAPTER TWO

Purposes of Case Studies

Case studies pose a problem or dilemma and are designed to help potential and practicing administrators

1. analyze various administrative problems;
2. identify feasible solutions to the problems;
3. examine the decisions they make and the bases on which they make them;
4. understand personal reactions to situations and to the people involved in them;
5. learn how to deal more thoughtfully and skillfully with the problems of relationships;
6. anticipate problems before they escalate and develop preventive strategies;
7. transfer learning in the classroom to real-life situations.

TYPES OF CASE STUDIES

The value of a case study depends upon the context in which it operates. A case study has no value apart from the context, which is both the key to understanding a case and applying it to new situations.

Case studies generally fall into the following categories:

1. An in-depth longitudinal history of a specific issue within a particular school district which can range from ten- to fifty- or more pages.

2. Five- to forty-page case studies of actual or fictionalized school districts, which give minute details and take several class sessions to adequately analyze and discuss.

  A. The longer case study typically provides rich detail about the context of the case.

  B. The chief purpose of the longer case study is to allow the reader to become immersed in the context described.

  C. Because of the rich detail and the intricacy of the relationships in the described context, it is more difficult to make a direct transfer to other contexts.

 3. The one-to two-page incident-targeted case study. Because of its length, more than one of this type of case study may be covered in a single class session in addition to, or as part of, the regular class lecture.

  A. A short case study typically provides minimal detail about the context of the case. These cases are vignettes of typical daily incidents in schools and describe only the incident, not its outcomes or ramifications. One suggested short case format includes a problem statement, background information, key questions, and suggested references.

  B. The short case supposes that the reader will apply additional details from one or more contexts with which he or she is familiar.

  C. There is a higher level of transfer because of the focused nature of this type of case study and less detail to assimilate and assess.

Selection of the case-study format is critical and depends on its intended use. Short case studies are excellent for stimulating different responses to a generic problem. The nature of the response is dependent upon the definition of the context by the user. Longer case studies are excellent for understanding a particular organization, serving as models for conducting in-depth studies of other organizations, identifying organizational models and specific roles, and increasing understanding of one's own organization.

  The cases in this book use the short-model format in order to allow professors to use one or more cases each week. These cases may serve as introductions to the lecture, as an inherent part of the content being presented, or as a culminating activity at the conclusion of the lesson. Students improve their ability to make decisions by "practicing" making many decisions rather than by addressing only a few cases during the semester.

CASE STUDY PROTOCOL

The protocol for developing short case studies should include an outline of the format for the case description, which includes the following sections:

1. Statement of the Problem. Within this section, the actual problem to be addressed is succinctly presented along with the facts required to understand the situation at hand.

2. Background Information. This section provides the reader with pertinent background data to help the reader understand what has occurred prior to the actual incident. The case study must provide sufficient information and evidence to allow those reading it to reach an independent judgment without additional information.

3. Case Study Questions. These include specific questions that direct the reader to focus on what the major issue really is, to identify what players must be dealt with and what outside sources must be consulted, and to make the reader aware of the complexity of the situation. Students need to spend time developing the questions, since the ability to ask the right questions is closely related to an individual's skill in thinking through problem situations and evaluating personal responses to this problem. Questions are intended to help the reader examine the various elements of the situation, to examine the characters and their relationships, to focus on the pressures and attitudes present, and to look at the ethical implications of alternative decisions.

4. References. This section contains additional sources that the reader can consult to gain further insight into the scope of the problem and identify alternative approaches used by others.

REASONS FOR THE POPULARITY OF THE CASE METHOD

The reasons behind the popularity of case studies are numerous. The major ones, however, may be summarized as follows.

Case studies
1. allow students to address problems that they might not have had the opportunity to encounter firsthand.

2. help students apply theoretical knowledge to actual situations by being actively involved in the lesson. When students become active, rather than passive, learners, they feel greater responsibility and ownership of the process and more effectively retain the concepts and principles presented.

3. assist students in sharpening their analytical and creative skills, as cases require careful thought.

4. provide students with the opportunity to refine their communication skills by presenting their ideas in class and by participating in group discussions where they have to defend their decisions.

5. involve students in team work, critical thinking, brainstorming, creative problem solving, shared decision making and the consequences of decisions.

6. simulate a situation by "doing," through such activities as role playing, debate and case discussion. Students often find it useful to role play the characters in the case study in order to view the problems from various vantage points.

7. allow students to react to demanding situations faced daily by administrators, which require them to quickly shift mental and emotional gears and learn how to handle many problems and projects at once.

8. provide time for essential reflection, analysis, and feedback in a safe environment. It is during this process that participants have the opportunity to validate, modify, or completely revise their positions by sharing with their colleagues. They can also apply various problem-solving approaches and analyze the problem again using different assumptions.

Case studies assist the student in integrating reality with theory in administrative preparation programs. Some of the theories taught in these programs include organization, social systems theory, management, leadership, decision making, communication, change, problem analysis, judgment, conflict resolution, role perception, and values and ethics. Case studies provide opportunities to review theory by applying it to the scenarios presented. Students are able to analyze how they make decisions, deal with conflict, consider problems, make assumptions, and rely on their biases, value systems, and past experiences as they develop and discuss case studies. Of necessity, students are forced to examine their beliefs, their style, and their way of operating in groups. They learn, in interacting with their peer group, that others also have good ideas about how to resolve problems, ideas that may differ from their own. Students can practice the skill of tactfully criticizing responses and also assess their own sensitivity level as others challenge their responses. They learn effective debating and negotiating skills in resolving problems and also learn how to work collaboratively. Students need to assess their interpersonal skills and their process skills. As they work with others in a shared decision-making setting, they begin to see that a group can formulate perhaps better solutions for problems that any one person can. As a result, they begin to identify and internalize strategies for involving faculty in the decision-making process when they become administrators. Cases include legal and supervisory issues to consider. Students also learn how to deal with ambiguity, since cases are open ended and usually do not provide solutions. It is crucial to develop all of these skills in training programs, because the number and nature of the problems faced by administrators on a daily basis prevent adequate time for reflection and analysis of each situation. In other words, administrators often must make frequent and instantaneous decisions, which requires prior practice. This practice is as essential to productive decision-making as constant practice is to any sport.

TRAINING STUDENTS TO USE CASE STUDIES

The following suggestions are offered for effective classroom use of case studies.

1. Make sure that the atmosphere or climate in which the case method is used is free and conducive to frank discussion of the cases. The leader and members of the group need to elicit the opinions and ideas of all the members and to insure that all have an opportunity to take part in the discussion. Since the students play a major role in the analysis and the decision making, the instructor provides the framework for case-study work and summarizes or redirects the discussion as necessary.
2. Consider the amount of time required by students to read, respond to, and present the case. Allow adequate time for thorough student analysis and discussion.
3. Assess the background of the students in terms of their ability to deal with the case-method approach and modify the amount of training accordingly.

4. Introduce case studies to the class at the first class meeting, review various types of cases, and describe the type of cases they will be using. In this book, all of the case studies are about actual teachers and other staff, most of whom are currently employed in schools. The names and places have been changed to insure the anonymity of the professionals, students, parents, and schools.

5. Inform the students that they will assume the role of the principal/administrator in analyzing and discussing these cases. Provide the option of having them role-play the characters. If this option is provided, the group should take a few minutes to think carefully about how the characters felt about the situation.

6. Address the fact that although some may be uncomfortable with the paucity of information in the case, in real life no one person knows everything about a particular situation. Different people have different pieces of information and consequently have a partial and therefore an incomplete view of the matter. As students seek to obtain additional data, they are refining their problem-analysis skills.

7. Tell the students that they will have adequate time for thorough case analysis and problem solving before making a decision in some of the cases. However, in several other cases, the students need to make a decision and take action immediately. This variation helps the students practice making carefully thought-out decisions and also sharpens their skills in crisis situations. In some cases, the principal has "inherited" a decision from another administrator, a decision that has created further problems.

8. Note that there are various vantage points that students can take in solving the case. Cases can often be solved several ways, depending on the position that the reader takes. Students can gain additional perspective by looking at "what exists" versus "what should exist."

9. Identify the need for students to draw upon the knowledge they have acquired in courses such as theories, supervision, school law, personnel, public relations, leadership, politics, curriculum and current issues.

10. Stress the need to assess the situation in the affective domain as well as the cognitive domain, as most problems involve people as well as decisions. Most case situations are not simple or

easily resolved; in fact, many of the situation outcomes depend upon the attitudes, feelings, and prejudices of the people involved.

11. Review the following fundamental rules.
    A. There is seldom a "correct" answer to any problem. Students should understand that there are usually several alternative ways to resolve any issue and should also know that there will be ambiguity in the process of case discussion.
    B. Reaching consensus is not the ultimate goal. It is more important to have students learn problem analysis, develop alternative strategies for dealing with the problem, and become able to predict what will happen if they choose one strategy over another.

CASE STUDY ANALYSIS SKILLS

Analysis is one of the least developed and most difficult aspects of case study use by students. In order to analyze cases in depth, the participants should have the following

1. The ability to identify the major issue(s) in the case study.
2. The ability to identify secondary issues for analysis and discussion.
3. The ability to interpret data.
4. The ability to develop a strategy and a set of procedures for analyzing the information in the case and to decide what is worth analyzing and how it should be done
5. Understanding of self and awareness of one's effect on others.
6. Effective listening skills, which requires observation and sensitivity to the nonverbal body language of the other group discussion members. It is important to be able to identify value screens (beliefs) and personal biases of the other participants and at the same time turn inward and reflect upon individual values and biases that "color" interpretation and decisions concerning the problem under discussion.
7. Adaptability and flexibility so that new situations will be viewed as opportunities, not threats to established value systems. Case studies have no right or wrong answers, and it is essential to be open to the views of the other discussants in order to expand an individual perspective.

8. The ability to deal with ambiguity. Problems in education are rarely clear cut, and students develop analytical skills by learning to deal with ambiguous situations.
9. Focus. It is important to stay on target and to assess the major problems and issues inherent in a particular case study without dealing with the extraneous issues that usually accompany any problem because of various groups often involved in any one incident.
10. Problem-analysis skills which allow a global understanding of the issues being studied.
11. Realistic expectations of the results of the actions taken to resolve the situation.
12. Lack of bias. Students need to understand that everyone filters information through their own value screen of personal reference. Case reviewers must not use a case study to substantiate a preconceived position.

MODELING CASE ANALYSIS AND DISCUSSION

1. Distribute a sample case study and have the participants read through the case before initiating analysis and discussion. Students may find it helpful to underline key ideas and make notes about what is happening.
2. Tell the students to identify first the major problems, then the secondary problems in the case. They should draw on their own knowledge, skills, and values. Have them list and rank the problems in writing, based on urgency or strategic importance. Then have them take notes about the symptoms versus the actual problems in the case.
3. Instruct the students to give careful thought to their own personal reactions to the case as well as to the point of view of each of the characters involved in the situation.
4. Inform the class that they are to prioritize the alternatives for each problem from most acceptable to least acceptable, briefly describing the strengths and weaknesses of each alternative. Individually, they should anticipate the consequences for each alternative. As a group, they are to recommend the most appropriate alternative for each problem based on the facts of the case and recognize the long-term implications of their decisions, which may need reassessment as further

developments occur. Sometimes there is a need for both immediate action and long-term action within the alternatives.

5. Have the students write responses to the questions at the end of the case.

6. Ask the students to share their responses. At this point encourage those who are comfortable with speaking to present their responses and allow those less comfortable to listen. However, at some point, the group needs to understand that everyone is expected to participate as the process continues, and the group works on its own.

7. After several group members have reported their ideas, the group should have the opportunity to think through and discuss the bases of these ideas. Ask some general questions regarding the basic problem or problems, whether additional information is needed, and, if so, how and where to find this information.

8. Help the participants analyze the responses and make sure that the proposed suggestions for action relate specifically to the problems in the case.

9. Discuss the steps necessary to implement each selected alternative for each problem identified, covering the "who, what, when, where" considerations.

10. Tell the students that there will be three levels of analysis for each case.

    A. The individual analysis. Each student reads, analyzes, and takes notes on a case prior to the small and large group meetings. This insures that each student will have studied the case, thought about its implications, and decided upon a course of action in advance of the class discussion.

    B. The small-group analysis. Divide the class into groups of approximately five to eight students. The teacher can appoint a discussion leader; the group can elect a leader, or the process can be conducted within a leaderless group. The advantage of dividing into groups is that all groups can discuss the same case simultaneously. Also, when a group works on a case, the variety of points of view on any one issue may be invaluable in demonstrating the surprisingly numerous ways of looking at a problem. Ideally, the group should have a heterogeneous membership, representing as many different perspectives as possible. Have the students share their individual analyses and suggestions with the rest of the group. Individual group members will provide feedback to each other and offer alternate suggestions and solutions based on their personal frame of reference. This shapes student behavior in the realm of teamwork as the students make decisions, think collectively, and work cooperatively toward the solution of a problem.

C. The large-group analysis. After the groups reconvene, each of the small groups will share their analysis and discussion of the case with the others. After the case has been analyzed and solutions presented, minority reports can be given by the individual group members describing alternative strategies for dealing with the problem. This summary activity further refines the students' problem-analysis skills as they discuss and debate the various solutions presented by the smaller groups. Students also gain a broad-based view and a heightened awareness of the difficulties inherent in the decision-making process.

11. Extend the debriefing session by having students discuss, where applicable, preventive measures that they might have taken to avoid or alter the situation before it escalated to this stage. Another purpose of these case studies is consideration of how to prevent problems from occurring or difficult relationships from becoming unbearable.

12. Understand that if a written case analysis is included, then the case study will require much more time. We believe that the value of the short case study is the ability to review a broad range of the problems that occur in schools and to be able to make multiple decisions carefully yet quickly, which is a skill required of all administrators.

CASE STUDY DEVELOPMENT

Case-study development helps aspiring administrators with reflective problem analysis. By writing cases about problems in their schools, students assess and internalize the multifaceted world of school administration. They begin to recognize the importance of working collaboratively with colleagues, learn how to identify and precisely explain complex problems faced by administrators, and develop preventive strategies to use when they become administrators. This assignment provides transfer, forcing students to write clearly and in a focused manner and helping them develop expertise in noting problems in real-life situations. School days do not usually allow time for talking and sharing with colleagues because everyone is tightly scheduled, but sharing cases (and eventually problems) with colleagues is an important aspect of professional development.

The following skills are commonly required for effective development of case studies.

1. The ability to identify an issue in their own school or educational workplace.
2. The ability to compose a case study based on personal knowledge of actual problems in an interesting, engaging manner. The student must acquire a clear style, one that constantly compels readers to continue reading and causes them to become enthusiastic about the material.
3. The ability to develop questions. Questions should not only focus the reader on the problem at hand but stimulate additional questions that expand the analysis and discussion. The questions should help the participants relate this one particular incident to their own work situation.
4. The ability to develop and discuss alternative perspectives. Each problem needs to be viewed according to the specific location, time, and people involved.

In addition to these skills, the writer of the case study must consider the following factors.

A. An initial draft of the case study should be written well before the assignment is due so that the student has time to reflect and revise the case study prior to submission. The writer should approach the case study as if it were a play, with action, emotional factors, suspense, and dialogue when appropriate.
B. The people and places described in the case must be assured anonymity. When an issue has involved a controversial topic, anonymity protects the real participants in the real situations.
C. The case study should have a quality of completeness. This characteristic is difficult to describe operationally: the problem statement has to provide a sense of the boundaries of the situation so that readers and discussants will immediately grasp an overall sense of the problem.

Have students draft a case study using the skills and considerations enumerated above. They need to keep in mind all that has been previously discussed and apply the concepts and principles learned in class to their case-study development. Then have them replicate the process of case-study analysis they have been using in analyzing and discussing prior cases.

CONCLUSION

Case studies are enjoying a new status in educational administration preparation programs throughout the United States and are an effective tool for conveying knowledge and analyzing behavior. Cases serve as catalysts for discussions about problem solving as they promote dialogue and interaction among prospective and practicing administrators. They stimulate reflections on personal leadership style and also present a framework for administrative problems and practices. Wasserman (1993) talks about "meaning making" and tells us that by ". . . mastering the basic clinical skills of observing, questioning, comparing and intuiting [we] can create personally appropriate ways of thinking about and acting on the problem of the moment." Students in educational administration programs need to become involved in the creative problem-solving process and develop a repertoire of skills in order to become effective future administrators.

REFERENCE

Wasserman, S. 1993. *Getting Down to Cases: Learning to Teach With Case Studies.* New York, NY. Teachers College Press.

CHAPTER THREE

Elementary-School Case Studies

Personnel problems in elementary schools are similar to those in middle schools, junior high schools, and high schools, with one significant difference. Most elementary schools are organized into self-contained classes, where one teacher teaches the students all day, every day, all year. Therefore, when a classroom teacher has a problem (e.g., alcoholism), the possible negative impact on each individual student is far greater than in the upper school levels, where students have classes with a teacher for only one or two periods per day. Students at the elementary level may not be aware of their teacher's problem(s), but the psychological impact may cause problems for them for many years to come. Elementary principals need to address quickly the immediate problem the teacher is having in order to avoid more complex, long-range problems involving students, parents, and community.

The cases presented in this section address a variety of problems with teachers including ineffective classroom management; problems of new teachers; teacher evaluation; accusations of physical, psychological, and sexual abuse; teacher personality; a teacher belittling students publicly; spreading confidential information to teachers; teacher-teacher affair; alcoholism and poor performance; teacher arrest; teacher death; teacher illiteracy; burn-out; placement after leave; termination; tenure recommendation; consolidation of classes; departmentalization; team-teaching conflict; poor field-trip management; and conflicting perceptions of curriculum; among others.

Cases dealing with parents include accusations of physical abuse by teachers; complaints about teachers' teaching; a request for student placement with a specific teacher; a demand to change teachers; a parent request to observe teachers; child custody issues; parent neglect;

an out-of-control parent; a parent's refusal to accept a retention decision; misuse of PTA presidential power; and an alleged sexual assault by a parent.

Student-focused cases include issues such as misbehavior on the school bus; classroom discipline problems; school phobia; school adjustment problems; drinking; stealing; and erratic behavior.

1. ALLEGED SEXUAL ASSAULT BY PARENT

Problem:

One of your teachers approached you in the hall the day after parent-teacher conferences. Quite distraught, she described an incident, as reported by a mother in her class, that occurred during a parent conference the night before. While the parents had been engrossed in the meeting, their pre-school child wandered into a vacant room. As the family was leaving the school, the child reported to her mother that a man had bothered her. "He was feeling my private parts," the girl reported, referring to her vagina. The man she was speaking of had been waiting with his son to speak to this teacher.

Background:

There is indication that the man in question is an alcoholic and had been asked earlier to please refrain from disturbing others. The mother was quite certain that her daughter's information was true. She mentioned quite hurriedly that she only mentioned this incident afterward because she hopes this man might be able to get some help. As principal, you need to sort out the significance of this incident. Circumstances that need to be considered are: the mother's not taking stronger action immediately and teachers who are generally upset about this incident.

Questions:

1. How will you respond to the parent's accusation?
2. What actions will you take with the accused man?
3. Whom should you consult about this matter?
4. What legal ramifications does this situation present?
5. How will you deal with the teachers who are upset?
6. How will you respond to possible concerns of other parents?

References:

Cohen, A. et al. 1996. Sexual harassment and sexual abuse: A handbook for teachers and administrators. ED396429.

Felon, M.J., and S.A. Mufson. 1994. A psychological first aid for children exposed to sexual violence. *School Counselor* 42:48-58.

Note: The use of an ED number (Clearinghouse Accession Number) in the reference list means that the document is not a journal article, but is one of the following other types of published and unpublished documents: research reports, curriculum and teaching guides, conference proceedings, project descriptions, and books. The following information is available when accessing an ERIC document through *RIE* or the Internet: abstract, accession number, author, availability, descriptors, identifiers, publication year, sponsoring agency, title, and pagination. A copy of the actual ERIC document is available at over 900 libraries that possess the ERIC microfiche collection or the ERIC document can be ordered on either paper or microfiche from the ERIC Document Reproduction Service. If a document is not available from ERIC because of copyright restrictions, the abstract will provide information on where to acquire a copy of the document.

2. CONFLICTING PERCEPTIONS OF KINDERGARTEN CURRICULUM

Problem:

Miss Parks is a kindergarten teacher. She enjoys her job and has taught in this community for over twenty-five years. Recently, parents have been complaining and requesting other teachers because Miss Parks doesn't teach academics to the kindergartners. Most of the children have been in nursery school for a minimum of one year, while some have as many as three years of preschool experience. Parents are very concerned that their children won't be ready in math or reading when they enter first grade. Some first-grade teachers have also been complaining that the children coming from Miss Park's class are academically behind in reading readiness, phonics, and math skills.

Background:

Miss Parks feels that kindergarten is a time for socialization and playing. She has many special play areas in the room and allows the children to play freely. Because of her huge body size, she rarely sits with the children or conducts formal lessons. She encourages children to come to her desk if they are doing a craft project or need her assistance. She is a very loving motherlike figure in the classroom and has a very high tolerance for both noise and clutter. When visiting, parents feel she is inadequate and they have expressed their concerns frequently to you, the principal. To meet some parents' demands, Miss Parks occasionally sends home a worksheet for homework, but she refuses to "teach" the skills.

Questions:

1. If you were going to confront this problem from an organizational perspective, what might you say to Miss Parks to drive home some basic instructional viewpoints?
2. How do you decide upon the right blend of socialization versus academics for kindergarten students?
3. How will you handle parents' requests?
4. Write an improvement plan for Miss Parks.

References:

Fromberg, D.P. 1995. The full-day kindergarten: Planning and practicing a dynamic themes curriculum. Early childhood education series. Second edition. ED386307.

Hill, P.S. 1992. Kindergarten. ED346995.

Karweit, N. 1992. The kindergarten experience. *Educational Leadership* 49:82-86.

McLean, S. Vianne et al. 1994. Kindergarten curriculum: Enrichment and impoverishment. *Early Child Development and Care* 101:1-12.

Schlak, L.E. 1994. Parents' and teachers' perceptions of the role of kindergarten in the educational process. ED383403.

3. CONSOLIDATION OF CLASSES DUE TO DOWNSIZING

Problem:

As of September 8, the second-grade class enrollment was 44. Ms. Sentor had 16 students, Ms. Jossey's class had a class size of 15 and Ms. Enfant's class size was also 15. The teachers were notified that if class enrollment did not increase by 17 students by Friday, September 12, one of the sections would have to be closed and the students would be consolidated into two classes. You, the principal, will decide who will remain as second-grade teacher and who will not.

Background:

Ms. Sentor has twenty-six years of service. Ms. Jossey has seventeen years of service. Ms. Enfant has only seven years of service. Ms. Sentor and Ms. Enfant work very closely together. On occasion, they even do some team teaching. Ms. Jossey empathetically expresses her desire to teach only the second grade. She knows second grade is her forte and wants to stay with what she knows best. It is also apparent that the other teachers want to stay in the second grade. You try to persuade each of them to accept a transfer, but no one volunteers. All three teachers have received satisfactory or above average evaluations. In addition, permission has been granted to open another section of fourth grade in the same building.

Questions:

1. How do you determine which class should be closed? What procedures must you follow in making this decision?
2. What impact does the negotiated contract have on this decision?
3. How will you work individually with the teacher who must move?
4. How do you fill the new fourth-grade position?
5. Write a memo to the parents whose children are affected.
6. How will you deal with the parents?

References:

Arrington, C.R. 1994. Education reform: How has downsizing affected the West Virginia school systems? ED379129.

Cochren, J.R. 1995. Leadership in an era of retrenchment. ED387905.

Fowler, W.J., Jr. 1992. What do we know about school size? What should we know? ED347675.

Raywid, M.A. 1996. Taking stock: The movement to create mini-schools, schools-within-schools, and separate small schools. Urban diversity series. No. 108. ED396045.

Williams, D.T. 1990. The dimensions of education: Recent research on school size. Working paper series. ED347006.

4. DEALING WITH PARENT NEGLECT

Problem:

Paul Smith is a learning-disabled fifth-grade student in a very affluent community. Two years ago he and his mother and sister were placed in the only low-income house in the community by social services because they were homeless. The Department of Social Services recently terminated their case with the Smith family, believing that the mother is acquiring income from illegal activities, including prostitution. The family will have to move out of the house and away from the community. The teachers, school counselor, and guidance people are concerned about the continuation of Paul's education, his emotional health, and his physical well-being.

Background:

Paul shows signs of depression and abuse. He will often carry his empty lunch bag to school pretending that it contains food. When the school counselor confronted the mother about burns found on Paul's hand, Mrs. Smith told the counselor that she was trying to teach Paul to iron. Paul's fifth-grade teacher went home with him after school one day and waited until midnight for the mother to appear. Mrs. Smith can be difficult and has often been unavailable for meetings.

Questions:

1. What steps can the school take to prepare Paul for his move?
2. Is there anything you can do about counseling Paul's mother?
3. How can teachers be sensitized to identify children whom they suspect are victims of abuse and neglect?
4. Whom should you consult regarding training programs for staff members?

References:

Cates, D.L. et al. 1995. At risk for abuse: A teacher's guide for recognizing and reporting child neglect and abuse. *Preventing School Failure* 39:6-9.

Chaffin, M. et al. 1996. Onset of physical abuse and neglect: Psychiatric, substance abuse and social risk factors from prospective community data. *Child Abuse & Neglect: The International Journal* 20:191-203.

Deisz, R. and others. 1996. Reasonable cause: A qualitative study of mandated reporting. *Child Abuse & Neglect: The International Journal* 20:275-287.

Gauthier, L. et al. 1996. Recall of childhood neglect and physical abuse as differential predictors of current psychological functioning. *Child Abuse & Neglect: The International Journal* 20:549-559.

Trocme, N., and C. Caunce. 1995. The educational needs of abused and neglected children: A review of the literature. *Early Childhood Development and Care* 106:101-135.

5. DECLINE IN TEACHING METHODS

Problem:

Mrs. Bush has taught at the same elementary school for twenty-seven years. When the district hired Mrs. Bush, she was married and the mother of five children. Her family lived in the community, and her children attended this school. For ten years, Mrs. Bush was a caring teacher whose lessons were innovative and interesting. During her tenth year of teaching, her style changed. Her lessons became mediocre and were directly from textbooks. Her students were assigned homework on lessons not taught in class. She experienced difficulty controlling her class, and her voice was often heard through her closed door. When parents requested their children not be in Mrs. Bush's class, it was usually honored. Every few years the former principal changed her grade level. Some parents have begun to complain to you, the new principal, about the excessive, often baseless homework. Others complain about her yelling at the pupils all the time.

Background:

Few were privy to the events that occurred in her life when her behavior became erratic seventeen years ago. Her husband became catastrophically ill. His condition continued to deteriorate until his death eight years ago. She still had young children to raise, and his illness took its toll on her. Nine years have passed. She is still experiencing difficulties in the classroom. She calls upon her peers to help her control her class. You have given her unsatisfactory evaluations the past two years.

Questions:

1. Identify the key issues in this case.

2. What should you do about Mrs. Bush? Provide assistance? Prepare disciplinary proceedings? Why?

3. Can intervention and assistance help a teacher who has veered so far " off course"?

References:

Doherty, K. 1995. A quantitative analysis of three teaching styles. *Journal of Experiential Education* 18:12-19.

Zahorik, J.A. 1991. Teaching style and textbooks. *Teaching and Teacher Education* 7:185-186.

6. ERRATIC STUDENT BEHAVIOR

Problem:

Mary Smith, a large, overweight fourth grader is having trouble adjusting to the present classroom situation. She has shown a complete disregard for authority, and does whatever she likes whenever she likes, exhibiting quite erratic behavior. She listens to the teacher and does some work when singled out, but reverts back to a negative attitude, refusing to do anything, when left to herself. During a lesson she will suddenly knock the books off a neighboring child's desk or throw crumpled paper at the teacher and the other students. At lunch or recess or during any unstructured period she hits or bothers the other children. Mary was recommended to the school psychologist and went for therapy but without much improvement. Her behavior has been getting steadily worse and the teacher has recommended that she be put in a special class. Her parents were contacted on several occasions but indicated that they did not want to be bothered.

Background:

Mary Smith is a fourth grade-student who is bused to this affluent elementary school along with other students from a poor neighborhood. Mary had gone to her neighborhood school from kindergarten until this year. The records indicate that she had been a problem since first grade but that nothing had been done about it. When the principal of the other school tried to remove Mary after a particularly bad incident, she sat down in the middle of the floor and refused to leave the classroom. No action was taken until May of that year when the child precipitated her own removal by attempting to strangle another child in the class. The child she tried to strangle was a child from her own neighborhood who she said teased her.

Questions:

1. As principal, how would you handle this problem with Mary?
2. How would you deal with Mary's parents?
3. Do you feel the problem would have occurred if the child was not bused to a new school?
4. Whom will you consult regarding this problem?

References:

Court, P. et al. 1995. Improving student behavior through social skills instruction. ED391579.

Horner, J. 1995. A student's right to protection from violence or sexual abuse by other students. *West's Education Law Quarterly* 4:110-114.

Johnson, L. et al. 1995. Improving student behavior. ED388398.

Rutherford, R.B., and M.C. Nelson. 1995. Management of aggressive and violent behavior in the schools. *Focus on Exceptional Children* 27:1-15.

Sussman, S. et al. 1994. Psychosocial variables as prospective predictors of violent events among adolescents. *Health Values: The Journal of Health Behavior, Education and Promotion* 18:29-40.

7. FINAL RECOMMENDATIONS FOR TENURE

Problem:

As of May 25, there are four elementary-school teachers whom Dr. McFadden, the superintendent, has not observed. He must observe these teachers before their final recommendation for tenure can be presented to the board of education on June 2. The teachers have no idea where they stand and they fear the superintendent will not observe them before the school year ends. One of them is getting married at the end of June and is literally tearing her hair out.

Background:

The Lawson School District hired Dr. McFadden in September. He observed the district for six months and it became obvious that he was ready to make major changes. The feeling in the district is that he intends to "have his way," regardless of the effect his decisions will have on faculty, staff, students, or parents.

Dr. McFadden initiated a policy that states that the superintendent will personally observe all teachers eligible for tenure and determine whether they will receive tenure. Furthermore, in April he was in the midst of reviewing other teachers for tenure recommendations and told three of them that he could not recommend them at that time based on items such as misspelled student work that was displayed on a bulletin board. It was later revealed that there were board-member objections to these particular teachers that explained why they were not recommended. He later recommended one of these teachers for tenure, one has never been told whether she will be recommended, and the third chose to leave the district.

Questions:

1. As principal of the elementary school, how will you handle this problem with the superintendent?
2. What are the legalities involved?
3. How will you work with the teachers on this issue?
4. What potential problems could occur if the superintendent continues to act in this manner?

References:

Behling, H.E., Jr. 1995. Recent legal decisions in education: A casebook of appellate court decisions-1985-1995. ED392113.

Mawdsley, R.D. 1991. Employees. ED340117.

Shreeve, W. et al. 1989. Teacher probation—an outdated concept? ED324281.

Ward, M.E. 1995. Teacher dismissal: The impact of tenure, administrator competence, and other factors. *School Administrator* 52:16-19.

8. ILLITERATE TEACHER

Problem:

Mrs. Gonzalez, a second-grade teacher on your staff, has a poor command of the English language and an even poorer command of Spanish, her native language. Although she has a very thick accent, that is not the cause of the difficulty. Native Spanish-speaking adults on the staff have difficulty understanding her in Spanish because her use of language structure and pronunciation are terrible. Her English diction is unclear and her syntax and usage are often incorrect. Blackboard writing, room signs, notes to parents, and corrections on children's work are frequently full of errors.

Although Mrs. Gonzalez is a lovely person who takes constructive criticism and suggestions for help willingly, she has no ability to transfer the suggestions and help to other situations and contexts. Her inability to communicate effectively affects not only the obvious, academic areas, but causes discipline and control problems as well.

Background:

Mrs. Gonzalez is an artistic, enthusiastic teacher and a caring woman. She is a devoted parent and carries many of her nurturing attitudes over to her class. She is licensed as a bilingual (Spanish-English) elementary teacher, but because of a need for regular education teachers in this poor, rural district at the time she was hired, she was placed in her present position and has received tenure in it. Several parents have recently requested that their children not be placed in her class next year.

Questions:

1. How would you as principal deal with Mrs. Gonzalez with regard to her incorrect written communication with children and parents? The need for her to take intensive and extensive English language training to upgrade her skills?
2. How will you respond to the parents' requests?
3. Whom will you consult regarding this matter?

References:

Crew, E., and P. Easton. 1990. Effective strategies for combating adult illiteracy. Annotated Bibliography. Adult literacy leadership project. ED330794.

Davis, S., and S. Diaz. 1994. Identifying and educating low-literate adults. *Reading Horizons* 34:316-323.

Giannangelo, D.M. et al. 1989. The whatever factor: Geographic literacy of teachers. *Journal of Social Studies Research* 13:34-39.

Schild, M. 1990. How to start an effective adult literacy program. ED330873.

Walsh, C. 1995. Twenty minutes a day keeps illiteracy away. ED394140

9. IMPACT OF TEACHER DEATH

Problem:

Mr. Roberts, a fifth-grade teacher, is killed on a Saturday evening in mid-May in a motorcycle accident. The school staff is called individually the next morning and asked to come in early on Monday for a meeting. The problems that exist are how to notify the students, counsel them and the staff, and what to do with the deceased teacher's scheduled class and classroom.

Background:

Mr. Roberts possessed a unique personality that enabled him to get along with, and be a role model for the school's students. He was a friend to the staff with whom he worked for fifteen years and served as vice president of the local teachers' union. In addition, he was a Vietnam veteran and worked part time with the local police department. He was a creative and free thinker, open to suggestions, empathetic, encouraging, and joyful.

Questions:

1. What internal sources will you consult in helping students and staff deal with Mr. Roberts' death?
2. What external sources will you call upon?
3. What will you do to help Mr. Roberts' class adjust to his loss and a new teacher?
4. How will you deal with the issue of bereavement in the future?

References:

Bereavement and loss manual: For administrators and teachers. 1992. ED344120.

Considine, A.S., and L.P. Steck. 1994. Working together: When death comes to school. ED3696334.

Crase, D.R., and D. Crase. 1995. Responding to a bereaved child in the school setting. ED394655.

Seibert, D. et al. 1993. Are you sad too? Helping children deal with loss and death. Suggestions for teachers, parents and other care providers of children to age 10. ED358398.

Walz, G.R., and J.C. Bleuer, eds. 1992. Helping students cope with fears and crises. ED340987.

10. INEFFECTIVE TEACHER EVALUATION

Problem:

You have formally evaluated Mrs. Gordon, a third-grade teacher in your elementary school for the second time this year. On both occasions you have indicated in writing that while she has prepared her lessons, used a variety of activities to teach concepts and to review skills, has circulated among the children, showed individual attention, and encouraged each child to work, there are a few "hard-to-reach" students who are not responding to her conscientious efforts. You have given her assistance during the year, and in addition transferred one child to another room. An attempt has been made to keep her class smaller than the other class at the same math level. You write the summative report, have her sign it, and send her home. The next morning you receive a scathing note in your mailbox from Mrs. Gordon stating that you are trying to destroy her reputation and are "out to get her."

Background:

Mrs. Gordon is an older teacher who has moved up the ranks from teacher's aide, to assistant, to teacher. She never completed student teaching under a sponsor teacher as it was waived. Prior to your arrival this year, all of her evaluations have always been excellent.

Questions:

1. How do you deal with Mrs. Gordon's anger?
2. How do you help Mrs. Gordon to be more effective? Develop a plan of action for her.
3. Write a memo responding to her note.
4. What other resources can you consult regarding this problem?

References:

Bearden, D. et al. 1995. Effective schools: Is there a winning combination of administrators, teachers, and students? ED386801.

Conley, D.T. 1991. Eight steps to improved teacher remediation. *NASSP Bulletin* 75:26-40.

Fuhr, D.L. 1993. Managing mediocrity in the classroom. *School Administrator* 50:26-29.

Miller, S. P. 1994. Peer coaching within an early childhood interdisciplinary setting. *Intervention in School and Clinic* 30:109-115.

Strube, M.J. 1991. Some rules for effective .and ineffective teaching: Generating lists as an educational exercise. *Teaching of Psychology* 18:174-176.

11. KINDERGARTEN RETENTION

Problem:

Mrs. Wilson is recommending a student for retention in kindergarten. The student is far behind the other students in the class both by teacher observation and the standardized Reading Readiness Test given to all kindergarten students each year in June. The teacher has had several conferences with both parents. The parents say they will not permit their child to be retained in the kindergarten. They claim that they will keep the child out of school all year if the student is retained.

Background:

Samantha has been consistently slow in adjusting to kindergarten. The student was five in August, so was chronologically where she belongs. Mrs. Wilson met with the parents twice during the first semester. In March a letter was sent home warning the parents that there was a possibility of retention. There was a meeting of the parents, teacher, and you, the principal. At that time the parents disagreed with you and the teacher, who felt that retention was in the best interest of the child. At the close of the meeting, the parents refused to sign a letter agreeing to this child's retention. Contact with the parents continued, but the parents refused to agree to the retention. Over the summer the parents came in and pleaded with you to place the child in first grade. They left the final meeting saying that they would not bring the child to school in September if she wasn't in first grade. One of the parents had gone through the school system and had been a slow learner. The other parent is unable to sign his name.

Questions:

1. Keeping in mind the best interests of the student, how would you handle this problem?
2. What factors need to be considered in making the best decision for this child?
3. What will you do if you retain the student and the parents keep their child home?
4. What are the laws in your state regarding this matter?

References:

Cosden, M. et al. 1993. The relationship of gender, ethnicity, and home language to age of school entry, kindergarten retention, and social promotion. ED364320.

Dennebaum, J.M., and J.M. Kulberg. 1994. Kindergarten retention and transition classrooms: Their relationship to achievement. *Psychology in the Schools* 31:5-12.

Mantzicopoulos, P., and D. Morrison. 1992. Kindergarten retention: Academic and behavioral outcomes through the end of second grade. *American Educational Research Journal* 29:182-198.

Sugzda, D. 1992. The effect of retention on kindergarten children. ED341972.

Zepeda, M. 1993. An exploratory study of demographic characteristics, retention, and developmentally appropriate practice in kindergarten. *Child Study Journal* 23:57-78.

12. LUNCH DUTY INCIDENT

Problem:

A child comes to you, with two student witnesses, to complain that a teacher pushed him against the wall in the yard during lunch. In addition, he claims that the teacher called him a " son of a bitch." When Mrs. Davis, the teacher, was called in, she admitted that she did call him a name but used the letter B, not the full word. She claims she did not touch the child, who had been very fresh to her.

Background:

Mrs. Davis is a competent teacher who is an asset to the school both in and out of the classroom. She was assigned to lunch duty, an undesirable assignment, and does a commendable job. She may have reached her frustration level at this time. She has been known to be confrontational with children.

Questions:

1. How will you resolve the situation before it becomes out of control?
2. How do you handle the witnesses?
3. How do you deal with alleged accusations of corporal punishment and abusive language?
4. To whom do you report this incident?

References:

Beckham, J.C. 1992. School officials and the courts: Update 1992. ERS Monograph. ED355621.

Rathbone, C.H., and R.T. Hyman. 1993. The regulation of corporal punishment: Examining the legal context in order to clarify the options for the small or rural school. ED362373.

13. MISUSE OF PTA PRESIDENTIAL POWER

Problem:

You are the newly hired principal of Park Elementary School. It is two weeks before the school opens and you are entering the building for the first time to go through files and organize for the opening of the school year. Your secretary is still on vacation.

As you walk through the front door you see a woman standing at the counter opening the mail. When you introduce yourself to her you find out that she is Mrs. Jarvis, the PTA president. You are somewhat surprised that she is opening and reading the mail and you tell her that you will be happy to take the mail and finish the job. She adamantly refuses and states that "sorting and opening the mail is my job."

Background:

You have replaced a principal who was at the school for sixteen years. He had "retired on the job," and in his last few years had neglected most of his administrative responsibilities. This allowed both teachers and parents to "take over" in areas that were completely inappropriate. You learn that the PTA has been trying to run the school and has succeeded in doing so in many areas. You know that parents should not be doing such things as reading school-district mail, but you are concerned about how to deal with this since you need the support of the PTA.

Questions:

1. What additional information do you need to have before you can solve this problem?
2. Who can help provide you with this information?
3. What actions should you take with Mrs. Jarvis?
4. How should you deal with the PTA on the issue of parent involvement?
5. What policies and procedures should you implement to insure that these practices do not continue?

References:

Belcastro, F.P. 1991. The PTA as a promoter of school community. *School Community Journal* 1:21-23.
Haar, C.K. 1995. Cutting class. The PTA plays hooky from educational reform. *Policy Review* 73:86-90.
Harden, G.D. 1993. Parents say the darndest things. *Principal* 72:40-41.
Inside your PTA. 1994. Awards for outstanding PTAs. *PTA Today* 20:37.

14. NEW TEACHERS AND CLASSROOM MANAGEMENT

Problem:

Ms. Summers was hired in September. She was assigned a fifth-grade class because of her prior experience with this grade level. From day one there were problems. The majority of her students were running through the halls disturbing other classes, while Ms. Summers taught to the three or four children who were still in the room. Teachers were constantly complaining of the noise, not only in the halls, but also coming from the classroom. Because of her lack of classroom management, she was assigned a mentor. While the mentor was in the room, students were on task and everything was fine. As soon as the mentor left the room, the chaos would begin. It was getting so bad that it was dangerous for the students to be in the room. You have spoken to her about this matter on several occasions. You have also documented these incidents for her file. It is now December and something must be done.

Background:

Ms. Summers gave a very impressive interview. She talked about her prior experience in a parochial school and her success there. Unfortunately, the school was closed as a result of budget cuts and her references could not be verified. She was hired anyway.

Questions:

1. Would you have hired Ms. Summers without verifying her references?
2. Since this is her first year in your district, what else would you do to provide assistance to her in addition to the mentor?
3. What would you do to insure improvement in her classroom management?
4. If she does not show improvement, what are the next steps?

References:

Barrett, E.R., and S.S. Davis. 1995. Perceptions of beginning teachers' inservice needs in classroom management. *Teacher Education and Practice* 11:22-27.

Burden, P.R. 1995. Classroom management and discipline: Methods to facilitate cooperation and instruction. ED387211.

Gibbons, L., and L. Jones. 1994. Novice teachers' reflectivity upon their classroom management. ED386446.

Martin, N.K., and B. Baldwin. 1994. Beliefs regarding classroom management style: Differences between novice and experienced teachers. ED387471.

Ralph, E.G. 1993. Beginning teachers and classroom management: Questions from practice, answers from research. *Middle School Journal* 25:60-64.

15. OUT-OF-CONTROL PARENT

Problem:

It is November of your first year as principal of Williams Elementary school. You are at a meeting in the superintendent's office when you receive a frantic phone call from your secretary. Mrs. Woods has stormed into the school office demanding to know the location of her child's sixth-grade classroom. Since there was not an administrator in the office, Mrs. Woods could not be stopped and she went to the classroom. As she stood in the doorway of the classroom, her daughter Christine let out a scream and jumped out of her seat. Mrs. Woods chased her daughter around the class and punched her with a closed fist whenever she could reach her. Finally three other teachers in that wing were able to persuade Mrs. Woods to leave the room. She is now sitting in your office.

Background:

This morning the assistant principal called Mrs. Woods to explain the girl's disruptive behavior yesterday. Christine has been giving the school a hard time since she transferred to Williams in September. Mrs. Woods has been notified several times during the past two months about Christine's negative behavior and has been cooperative. Christine's records did not indicate any trouble in prior years at her former school. However, in September Christine's mother was released from prison for killing her boyfriend several years ago.

Questions:

1. How will you handle Mrs. Woods?
2. What assistance will you provide to Christine?
3. What outside agencies will you contact regarding this incident?
4. What types of safeguards will you initiate in order to prevent violent parents and unknown intruders from entering classrooms?

References:

Boutte, G.S. et al. 1992. Effective techniques for involving "difficult" parents. *Young Children* 47:19-22.

McCree, W.S. 1995. Helping parents deal with the discipline of their children through a parenting support group. ED387237.

Nweke, W.C. et al. 1994. Racial differences in parental discipline practices. ED388741.

Schwab, N. 1994. Discipline: Reflections on parenting. *Montessori Life* 6:11.

Straus, M.A., and D.A. Donnelly. 1993. Corporal punishment of adolescents by American parents. *Youth and Society* 24:419-442.

16. PARENT ACCUSATION OF PHYSICAL ABUSE BY TEACHER

Problem:

Mrs. Taylor has been employed as a fourth-grade teacher for twelve years in the Waterman Elementary School. There is one other fourth grade class in the building and often the two classes join together for recess and lunch. The teachers alternate days supervising the classes during these noninstructional times.

During one recess, Tom, a student, began to use profanities while talking to another child. Mrs. Taylor was on duty and asked him to stop. Tom continued to curse and Mrs. Taylor told him that she would wash his mouth out with soap if he did not stop. Tom continued to swear and Mrs. Taylor physically removed him from the playground. She brought him inside to the girl's bathroom and allegedly washed his mouth out with soap.

Tom went home that afternoon and reported the events to his parents. His parents called the school to speak with the teacher. The teacher had already left the building and as a result, the parents spoke to you, the principal. You were unaware of this event, but assured the parents you would speak to the teacher and determine exactly what had transpired. The parents, outraged by the actions of the teacher, called the media and demonstrated in front of the school the next day, carrying a sink. They have hired legal counsel and have sued the teacher and the school district.

Mrs. Taylor has denied actually putting soap in Tom's mouth. She admitted to having put soap from a dispenser in the girl's bathroom on her finger and then placing her finger near Tom's mouth.

Background:

Mrs. Taylor's observations and evaluations for the past twelve years have all been satisfactory. There is no documented evidence that behaviors like this have ever occurred in the past. Many teachers in the district who have worked with Mrs. Taylor, however, claim that she has washed children's mouths out with soap on many occasions; however, there is no documented evidence, only hearsay.

Tom's parents have a long history of taking legal actions; they have sued the physician who delivered Tom and the hospital for negligence, claiming they are the cause of Tom's learning disabilities.

Questions:

1. How can you find out what actually happened between Tom and Mrs. Taylor?
2. If Mrs. Taylor did put soap in Tom's mouth, what actions will you take?
3. How will you deal with Tom's parents?
4. Since the parents have initiated legal proceedings, who in the district can you turn to for assistance?

References:

Crow, N.A. 1991. Personal perspectives on classroom management. ED332959.

Reisberg, L. et al. 1991. Classroom management: Implementing a system for students with BD. *Intervention in School and Clinic* 27:31-38.

Sprick, R.S., and L.M. Howard. 1995. The teacher's encyclopedia of behavior management: 100 problems/500 plans for grades K-9. ED386887.

Swick, K.J. 1991. Discipline: Toward positive student behavior. What research says to the teacher. ED335135.

Thomas, S.B., and C.J. Russo. 1995. Special education law: Issues and implications for the 90s. ED392114.

17. PARENT COMPLAINT ABOUT TEACHER

Problem:

John Anderson, a second grader, refused to sit down yesterday afternoon during a science lesson presented by his teacher. After repeated requests to sit down and John's repeated refusals to do so, the teacher made him stand outside the room in the corridor and forgot completely that he was there.

This morning Mrs. Anderson came into the office demanding to see you, the principal. She angrily told you all the things that she felt were incorrectly done by the teacher in the classroom and stated that this teacher's services in the school should be terminated. If that could not be accomplished, then her son must be placed in another class.

Background:

John's mother is always in and around the school as a parent volunteer. She keeps tabs on her son by looking in the door of his classroom at every possible opportunity to make sure that he is not annoyed by anyone. John cries easily and frequently accuses others of starting fights with him or annoying him. Mrs. Anderson saw her son standing outside his classroom yesterday and she is furious.

Questions:

1. What action would you take with the teacher who sat the child outside the classroom and forgot about him?
2. How do you explain to the parent that the teacher's actions are not serious enough to terminate the teacher?
3. What kind of counsel do you give a parent whose child is always misbehaving?
4. How do you tell an overinvolved parent that her constant presence in the school is distracting to teachers and students?

References:

Kennedy, C. 1990. The ups and downs of school-parent relations. *School Administrator* 47:22-24.

Motsinger, H.M. 1990. Positive parent involvement is possible if   ED337332.

Roeser, R.W. et al. 1995. A longitudinal study of patterns of parent involvement in schools across the elementary years. ED385382.

18. PARENT DEMAND TO CHANGE TEACHER

Problem:

Mrs. Jackson's son, Joseph, is in the third grade. Yesterday, February 10, Mrs. Jackson came to school for a conference with you, the principal. At that time she claimed that her son was gifted and that the group IQ test score of 124 was too low. She requested that an individual IQ test be administered to her son. In addition she felt that he wasn't being challenged in his classroom and demanded that he be changed immediately to another, which she specifically named. She was aware of the school policy that is opposed to moving children at midyear, but she could not be persuaded of the problems involved in making such a change. Mrs. Jackson threatened to take the problem over your head to the superintendent and the school board until she was satisfied.

Background:

You have met with Mrs. Jackson several times this year to help her find an appropriate placement for her autistic four-year-old daughter, so you assumed this meeting was a continuation of that discussion. She exerts strong pressure on Joseph, who is personally very self-motivated but is also "uptight" and anxious to fulfill his own and his mother's expectations. His classroom performance is average to above average, but in his haste to finish an assignment in order to do more than the other students, he makes frequent and careless mistakes.

Questions:

1. What is your immediate response to Mrs. Jackson?
2. Describe your conversation with the superintendent regarding this matter.
3. What information will you seek from the teachers and school psychologist?
4. How will you provide assistance to Joseph to help him overcome his "uptight" behavior?

References:

Conderman, G., and A. Katsiyannis. 1996. State practices in serving individuals with autism. *Focus on Autism and Other Developmental Disabilities* 11:29-36.

Gelfer, J.I. 1991. Teacher-parent partnerships: Enhancing communication. *Childhood Education* 67:164-167.

Mesibov, G.B., and V. Shea. 1996. Full inclusion and students with autism. *Journal of Autism and Developmental Disorders* 26:337-346.

Smith, S.E. 1994. Parent-initiated contracts: An intervention for school-related behaviors. *Elementary School Guidance and Counseling* 28:182-187.

Stone, W.L., and K.L. Hogan. 1993. A structured parent interview for identifying young children with autism. *Journal of Autism and Developmental Disorders* 23:639-662.

19. PARENT REFUSAL TO ACCEPT SCHOOL RETENTION POLICY

Problem:

Closing-Day exercises have just been completed and the school year is officially over. Most of the children have left with their parents. You return to your office. Mrs. Barnes, the mother of a child who has just completed the second grade, strides into your office, shuts the door, and says she must see you right now. She has just discovered a letter enclosed in her daughter Joan's report card saying that the child is to be retained in the second grade. This was the first time she had ever heard of the idea and it was the last straw! There had been many things with which she had been dissatisfied during the school year. She knew the teacher had not understood Joan and really hadn't taken that much interest in her or given her much help. Maybe they would have to take Joan out of the school.

Background:

You, as principal, had approved the letter when the teacher presented it to you the week before. The teacher assured you that she and the reading teacher had informed the father of this recommendation at the April parent conference. You know that other than the April conference, most contact during the year had been with the mother; that a great deal of extra time and effort had gone into helping this child during the year; that testing at the local hospital's screening program had revealed some serious learning and perceptual problems; that the teachers who had worked with Joan were concerned with the parents' lack of understanding of her capabilities and their unwillingness to spend extra time with her. They were also concerned about her placement for next year.

Questions:

1. How do you handle the mother?
2. What procedures do you follow with the child's teacher?
3. Is retention an acceptable alternative for a learning-disabled child?
4. How do you prevent situations like this from happening in the future?

References:

Alexander, K.L. et al. 1994. On the success of failure: A reassessment of the effects of retention in the primary grades. ED387203.

Byrd, R. S., and M.L. Weitzman. 1994. Predictors of early grade retention among children in the United States. *Pediatrics* 93:481-487.

Tanner, C. K., and E.F. Combs. 1993. Student retention policy: The gap between research and practice. *Journal of Research in Childhood Education* 8:69-77.

Turco, A. 1993. Reducing the retention rate among kindergarten, first-and-second grade students. ED371820.

Walters, D.M., and S.B. Borgers. 1995. Student retention: Is it effective? *School Counselor* 42:300-310.

20. PARENT REQUEST TO OBSERVE TEACHERS

Problem:

Early this spring, you, the principal of Malden Elementary School, received a request from Mrs. Cronin, a parent. She wants to come to school and "sit in and observe all the first-grade teachers." Since Mrs. Cronin has a child in kindergarten, her goal is to evaluate the teachers and then to make a request for her child's placement next year with the teacher of her choice. The teachers are upset and state that it is a violation of their contract.

Background:

Malden has traditionally had a policy that parents are always welcome to observe programs and classes in action. This is an upper-middle-class community where parents take an active part in school affairs. Mrs. Cronin made the same request last year to evaluate kindergarten teachers and requested the teacher she thought her son should have when he entered school. Your predecessor honored her request.

Questions:

1. Should a principal honor requests from parents for a specific classroom teacher?
2. What problems might occur if the principal honors these requests?
3. What happens if the principal does not honor requests?

4. Does the teachers' contract present an ethical dilemma in denying taxpayers access to schools?
5. Should a school have a policy governing parent visitations and observations?

References:

Bempechat, J. 1992. The role of parent involvement in children's academic achievement. *School Community Journal* 2:31-41.
Parent involvement in education: A resource for parents, educators, and communities. 1994. ED387245.

21. PARENTAL REQUESTS FOR KINDERGARTEN PLACEMENT

Problem:

The parents at Hutton School, specifically those having children about to enter kindergarten, are in an uproar. In the past, the building principal has "graciously" granted their specific teacher requests. You, the recently hired principal, have grave reservations about this practice. You do not think these requests should be honored. The parents threaten, "If our requests are not honored, we'll go to the superintendent."

Background:

Ms. Moore has been teaching kindergarten for fifteen years. (There are two other kindergarten teachers in the building.) She has established an excellent reputation. Her rapport with parents has been outstanding. Her children consistently score well on first-grade placement tests. For years, over 50 percent of the parents have been requesting Ms. Moore to be their child's kindergarten teacher. Their requests have always been honored. As a result, Ms. Moore consistently ends up with the "best" children, making the other two kindergarten teachers feel resentful.

Questions:

1. Should you honor parent requests for specific teachers?
2. What problems occur when this practice occurs?

3. What problems occur when the principal does not honor parent requests?
4. If you decide not to honor the parent requests, how will you notify the parents?
5. How will you ease the resentment of the other two kindergarten teachers?

References:

Ames, C. et al. 1995. Teachers' school-to-home communications and parent involvement: The role of parent perceptions and beliefs. Report No. 28. ED383451.

Bobango, J.C. 1994. Promoting parent involvement: Because educators can't do it all. *Schools in the Middle* 3:26-28.

Ribas, W.B. 1993. Parents offer 10 tips for communicating with teachers. *PTA Today* 19:13.

22. PHYSICAL ABUSE BY TEACHER

Problem:

Ms. Bundy is a fifth-grade teacher who is unable to maintain control in any class she teaches. The students run around the room and several fights break out every day. Ms. Bundy loses her temper and has been warned about saying threatening things to the children. Three years ago when she was teaching a second-grade class, three mothers complained to you, the principal, that she had hit their children with several objects, including a pointer and her shoe. Several other children complained that Ms. Bundy had hit them with books. Ms. Bundy denied having hit the children, and since the parents were unwilling to press charges, she was given a warning and a letter in her personnel file. Now parents have complained several times to you about her physical and verbal abuse. You want to initiate a district investigation, but you have no concrete evidence and no adult witnesses. Once again, the parents are not willing to press charges against Ms. Bundy but want you to "do something."

Background:

Ms. Bundy is a tenured teacher with fifteen years experience in a large urban school district. She has been transferred from school to school for the last twelve years because she is unable to maintain classroom control. She has been brought up on charges of physical and verbal abuse several times in several schools, but she grieved through the union grievance policy each time and had the letters of reprimand pulled from her file. She has been at her present assignment for two years, the longest time she has served in any one school. The district superintendent has informed you that Ms. Bundy will remain at your school if an acceptable transfer cannot be arranged.

Questions:

1. How can Ms. Bundy be prevented from hurting any more children?
2. What can be done about this whole situation?
3. What contractual and/or legal ramifications must be considered in dealing with Ms. Bundy?
4. Write an improvement plan for Ms. Bundy.

References:

Camp, W. E., Ed., et al. 1993. The principal's legal handbook. ED354606.

Fossey, W.R. 1990. Confidential settlement agreements between school districts and teachers accused of child abuse: Issues of law and ethics. *West's Education Law Reporter* 63:1-10.

Hooker, C.P. 1994. Terminating teachers and revoking their licensure for conduct beyond the schoolhouse gate. ED379754.

Lawrence, C. E., and M.K. Vachon. 1995. How to handle staff misconduct: A step-by-step guide. ED377569.

Pearce, A.C. 1992. Investigating allegations of inappropriate physical punishment of students by school employees. *School Law Bulletin* 23:15-21.

23. POOR FIELD TRIP MANAGEMENT

Problem:

All the first-grade classes in Hagen Elementary School left for a field trip to the zoo. Each bus held two classes, two teachers, several parents and many students. Two buses out of three returned to school on time. The third bus was more than halfway home before the new teacher realized her colleague and several students were missing from the bus. She asked the bus driver to return to the zoo. The bus driver contacted the bus garage dispatcher who called you, the principal. Upon their arrival back in the school you spoke to the four experienced returning teachers and inquired how they could have left the zoo before checking to see that the third bus was also ready to return, with all staff, parents, and children.

Background:

The staff of this school is almost entirely made up of older experienced teachers. In recent years, only a handful of younger and relatively inexperienced teachers have been assigned to the faculty. The principal has just been granted tenure and is often referred to as "the young boy." Often, he is told "this is how we have done things for 'x' amount of years" and "why change something that works?" In the past, even though there was always a grade-level field trip, each bus came and left independently of the others. Each teacher was responsible for her own class and the parent chaperones.

Questions:

1. How could a principal best voice his concern for the safety of all staff and students?
2. How could this and similar situations be corrected and prevented in the future?
3. What action is necessary to take with the new, nontenured teacher who rode the bus for twenty minutes before realizing her colleague and students were missing?
4. How can the knowledge gained from this case study be applied to other personnel issues?

References:

Cox, C.C. III. 1993. The field trip as a positive experience for the learning disabled. *Social Education* 57:92-94.

Hawke, D. 1991. Field trips and how to get the most out of them. *Pathways* 3:16-17.

Smith, R.A. 1995. Personal and professional traits that influence hiring of beginning teachers. *Journal of Technology Studies* 21:47-56.

Warner, J. et al. 1995. The unauthorized teacher's survival guide. Ed383691.

Wyatt, L.D. 1996. More time, more training. *School Administrator* 53:16-18.

24. PRINCIPAL INVOLVEMENT IN CHILD-CUSTODY ISSUES

Problem:

The Tompkins family has two children in the Lincoln Elementary School. Heidi is in a morning kindergarten class and Jim is in fourth grade. Their parents recently separated. The mother has legal custody but the father has visitation rights. Mrs. Tompkins has asked you, the principal, not to allow the father to pick up or see the children. She has also asked you to have the teachers of both children write letters about the children's adjustment in school. The letters are to be addressed "to whom it may concern." Mr. Tompkins has asked to pick up the children on several different occasions. He also wants to speak to them during school hours. Mrs. Tompkins wants the letters. The teachers want to know what is happening.

Background:

Several times during the past month no one has been home to meet Heidi at 11:45 a.m. On two occasions the bus driver brought her back to school. The parents are in a custody fight in which Mr. Tompkins is accusing his wife of improper child care. There is a two year old at home whom the father recently "kidnapped." The police were involved and the baby was returned home in 24 hours. Mr. Tompkins owns the home that the three children and Mrs. Tompkins are living in. Both children are doing well in school. Financially, the family is upper middle class.

Questions:

1. What role should the school play in child custody issues?
2. What legal requirements must you follow in dealing with both Mrs. Tompkins and Mr. Tompkins?
3. Should children's protective services be consulted?
4. How will you respond to Mr. and Mrs. Tompkins' requests?

References:

Austin, J.F. 1991. The impact of school policies on noncustodial parents. ED338971.

Bartlett, L.D. 1994. School administrators and law enforcement officials. Legal memorandum. ED371467.

Kurtz, L. et al. 1993. Access by noncustodial parents: Effects upon children's postdivorce coping resources. ED371266.

Tarriff, H.M., and V. Levine. 1993. Involving divorced parents. *Principal* 73:37-38, 40.

Trotter, A. 1993. Shutting out child-snatchers. *American School Board Journal* 180:28-30.

25. PROBLEMS WITH DEPARTMENTALIZATION IN ELEMENTARY SCHOOLS

Problem:

Miss Egan is a sixth-grade teacher at Lawrence Elementary School. She has ten years of teaching experience and recently transferred to Lawrence from Golden Elementary because of redistricting. Miss Egan teaches reading and language arts to her homeroom class. The class changes location and teachers for arithmetic and science. There is little communication between Miss Egan and the other two sixth-grade teachers. In fact, the sixth-grade program is more departmentalized in nature as a team approach is not used.

Two months after school opened, Miss Egan assigned a thirty-page report to all her students. You received numerous calls from parents complaining about the size of the assignment. Miss Egan sent a note home explaining the assignment more fully. She assured parents that she would guide the children through the assignment and even spend time after school with them if necessary.

When the first report card came out, Miss Egan failed 66 of 91 children in her classes. Again, the parents called. You scheduled a meeting with the sixth-grade teachers. Miss Egan was absent the day of the meeting. The other two sixth-grade teachers, Mr. Leplant and Mrs. Stevens, met with you and discussed the possibilities of ending the departmentalized program at midyear, at the end of the year, or immediately. The next morning, Mr. Leplant told Miss Egan what was discussed. That afternoon Miss Egan sent a note home to parents stating beginning Monday all sixth-grade classrooms would be self-contained.

Background:

The sixth-grade program at Lawrence has been a departmentalized program for the past six years. Over this period of time, Mr. Leplant, the science teacher, is the only person to remain in the same position. The social-studies position has been held by three different teachers; the math position by four. Miss Egan, whose previous experience had been in a sixth-grade, self-contained classroom, had accepted her present position with some degree of apprehension. At the interview, Miss Egan stated that while she was used to teaching in a self-contained class, a new experience would be interesting and enlightening. When told about the lower socioeconomic status of the children at Lawrence as compared to Golden, Miss Egan assured the principal that she would not encounter a problem in this area. "I come from a similar background and know what it's like to have a tough time in school and elsewhere. I have my standards and stick to them; but I am also ready to help anyone who is finding the going rough."

Questions:

1. Often staff members hide problems behind a false sense of standards. They say, "I have my standards," as a way of rebuffing a need for flexibility. In what way do "standards" get in the way of solving problems?
2. Specifically, what are Miss Egan's problems? Make some notes that pinpoint the problems and that suggest some solutions.
3. Do Miss Egan and her colleagues have any sense of teaming? How would you fix the problems?
4. How will you deal with the notes that Miss Egan sent home to parents?

References:

Ediger, M. 1994. Grouping pupils for language arts instruction. ED369066.

Harris, M.B. 1996. The effect of departmentalization on the reading achievement of sixth-grade students. ED395298.

Husband, R.E., and P.M. Short. 1994. Middle school interdisciplinary teams: An avenue to greater teacher empowerment. ED372043.

MacIver, D.J., and J.L. Epstein. 1993. Middle grades research: Not yet mature, but no longer a child. *Elementary School Journal* 93:519-533.

Malecki, C.L. 1990. Teaching whole science: In a departmentalized elementary setting. *Childhood Education* 66:232-236.

26. SCHOOL PHOBIA

Problem:

Howard Smith, a new fourth-grade student at Thomas Jefferson Elementary School, is a school phobic. He is unable to spend more than one or two hours at school. His mother and father are constantly on call and spend many days sitting in the car in the school parking lot in case Howard has to be taken home. Howard is unable to eat lunch in the cafeteria and does not want to play with the other children at recess. Mrs. Gallin, Howard's teacher, is having extreme difficulty dealing with the problem. Howard spends most of his time in school in the psychologist's office.

Background:

Howard's family has moved several times. He has attended three different elementary schools. Howard is also dealing with a new baby in the family. He experienced similar problems at the last school he attended. Last year at his previous school, six months passed before he was able to attend on a regular basis.

Questions:

1. How would you respond to this situation?
2. Would you refer Howard for psychological testing?
3. Are there behavior-modification programs that can be used to help school-phobic students?
4. How should the principal deal with the parents?

References:

Deluty, R.H., and J.L. DeVitis. 1996. Fears in the classroom: Psychological issues and pedagogical implications. *Educational Horizons* 74:108-113.

Kearney, C.A. et al. 1995. The legend and myth of school phobia. *School Psychology Quarterly* 10:65-85.

Kearney, C.A., and J.F. Beasley. 1994. The clinical treatment of school refusal behavior: A survey of referral and practice characteristics. *Psychology in the Schools* 31:128-132.

Paige, L.Z. 1993. The identification and treatment of school phobia. Publication No. 6503. ED366863.

Phelps, L. et al. 1992. School phobia and separation anxiety: Diagnostic and treatment comparisons. *Psychology in the Schools* 29:384-394.

27. SPREADING CONFIDENTIAL DISTRICT INFORMATION TO TEACHERS

Problem:

The fifth-and sixth-grade coordinator in the Glenbrook School has been making decisions without your approval. Frequently these decisions are contradictory to your wishes. As a result, teachers are often getting two varied sets of directives, which causes great conflict. The coordinator is permitted to make administrative decisions as part of her job description. There is a definite power struggle between you and the coordinator at present. The coordinator has also been spreading confidential district information to various teachers. This information, although often accurate, has been causing dissension among teachers.

Background:

Glenbrook School is a modified open-concept school with a warm, cohesive faculty. Morale is high in this building. The coordinator serves half time and teaches the remainder of the day. She has been admired for her skills during her twelve years of teaching. She is an extremely dominant and forceful individual. She is also quite opinionated. You are highly respected by your staff and you deal with them in a warm and humanistic manner.

Questions:

1. How do you inform the coordinator that sharing confidential information is a breach of ethics?
2. Why should the coordinator not be permitted to behave so unprofessionally?
3. What problems are created when staff members engage in power struggles with administrators?
4. Write a memo to the coordinator that directs her to stop the bad behavior immediately.

References:

Beeson, G.W., and R.J. Matthews. 1993. Collaborative decision making between new principals and teachers: Policy and practice. ED361837.

Decision-making process. Annotated bibliography of tests. 1991. ED369830.

Ferrara, D.L., and J.T. Repa. 1993. Measuring shared decision making. *Educational Leadership* 51:71-72.

Liontos, L.B. 1994. Shared decision-making. ERIC Digest. ED368034.

Smith, C.B. 1991. Teacher as decision-maker. ED326850.

28. STATUS OF PSYCHOLOGICAL REFERRAL

Problem:

About two weeks into January, Mr. Green, the head delegate to the teachers' union, met with you, the principal, to discuss a problem presented to him by Mrs. Jones, a third-grade teacher. Mrs. Jones was very concerned about the status of a psychological referral she submitted in late November. Mr. Green asked you if psychological referrals were being acted upon in a timely manner, since there is a law that a child shall receive this service within thirty days.

Background:

Mrs. Jones had found the referral file of one of her students under a pile of papers in the health room. Mrs. Jones also told Mr. Green that a sixth-grade teacher completed a referral in early October, which has also not been processed. Mrs. Jones states that only one student in the regular classes has been seen by the psychologist, while he has seen thirteen students with handicapping conditions.

Questions:

1. How would you handle the problem presented by Mr. Green?
2. What are the underlying problems that need your attention? List them in order of priority.
3. How will you find out whether Mrs. Jones' accusations are true?
4. Why was Mrs. Jones going through the pile of papers in the health room? What will you say to her about this?

References:

Horvath, M.J. et al. 1991. Special education and the law. ED345411.

Kastner, J., and J. Gottlieb. 1991. Classification of children in special education: Importance of pre-assessment information. *Psychology in the Schools* 28:19-27.

Reschly, D.J. 1996. Identification and assessment of students with disabilities. *Future of Children* 6:40-53.

Safran, S. P. et al. 1991. Special education classification and program success: Is there a relationship? *Psychology in the Schools* 28:340-345.

Wisniewski, J.J. et al. 1995. Objective and subjective factors in the disproportionate referral of children for academic problems. *Journal of Consulting and Clinical Psychology* 63:1032-1036.

29. STUDENT ADJUSTMENT PROBLEMS

Problem:

Mrs. Sullivan's daughter, Kathryn, is in a small first-grade class. On December 20, a group meeting was held with Mrs. Sullivan to discuss Kathryn's pronounced adjustment problems. Her behavior often takes on bizarre characteristics. Those present at the meeting were you, the school principal; the classroom teacher; the resource-room teacher; and the school psychologist. On three previous occasions, Mrs. Sullivan canceled scheduled appointments at the last minute. Mrs. Sullivan feels that Kathryn does not like school nor does she want to attend. Furthermore, Mrs. Sullivan feels Kathryn has some type of personality conflict with her classroom teacher and requested that her daughter be placed in another, specifically named, first-grade class. The classroom teacher, resource-room teacher, and school psychologist are adamantly opposed to Kathryn's class change. You decide to honor Mrs. Sullivan's request and change Kathryn's class on a trial basis on the condition that the Sullivans seek additional outside medical and neurological evaluations. Mrs. Sullivan agrees to do so. After several weeks, this placement was to be evaluated and another conference set up between the school staff members and Mr. and Mrs. Sullivan. So far there have been no follow-up evaluations or inquiries for outside help by Kathryn's parents.

Background:

In kindergarten, Kathryn did not communicate. She lacked verbal interaction and reaction to her peers. Kathryn can, however, work well on a one-to-one basis when she understands what to do. This behavior has continued in first grade. There is a degree of withdrawal and noninvolvement. She rarely participates in activities in the classroom or outside. Three special teachers could not even evaluate her on report cards due to her total unresponsiveness. The school psychologist spent eight sessions with Kathryn to secure a valid evaluation. Kathryn is enrolled in a maximum resource-room program to work on class work, auditory skills, group participation, and coping with classroom situations. Mrs. Sullivan thinks Kathryn will grow out of this. Mrs. Sullivan is frequently away from home, either working part-time or going to school for a master's degree in special education. In fact, when she comes for a conference, she carries her books along with her.

Questions:

1. How would you make the Sullivans realize that a severe problem does exist?
2. How would you persuade the Sullivans of the necessity of seeking additional outside help?
3. What would be your next step in dealing with Mr. and Mrs. Sullivan?

References:

Butera, G. et al. 1994. Classroom behaviors of students in rural mainstreamed settings: A comparison of students with disabilities and their normative peers. ED369605.

Hartwig, R.P., and G.M. Ruesch. 1994. Disciplining students with disabilities: A synthesis of critical and emerging issues. Final report. Project FORUM. ED378712.

McKinney, J.R. 1993. Special education and parental choice: An oxymoron in the making. *West's Education Law Review* 2:46-56.

Sorensen, G. 1995. Discipline of students with disabilities: An update. ED384192.

Thomas, S.B., and C.A. Denzinger. 1993. Special education law: Case summaries and federal regulations. ED378765.

30. STUDENT DISCIPLINE ON SCHOOL BUS

Problem:

More than one-half of the discipline referrals submitted on students in Taft Elementary School are the result of inappropriate student behavior on the school bus. Handling these referrals often takes a major portion of your day. The situation on the buses places children in jeopardy and does little to encourage them to arrive at school "ready to learn."

Background:

Taft is a large elementary school in one of the county's largest school districts. More than 1,100 students in grades K-6 are served at this site. Since this school is one of several "theme" schools, students are enrolled as a result of parental choice. This means that for some of the students, the bus ride is forty-five minutes each way. Bus transportation, provided by two different companies using twenty-two buses for a single run, is provided for all students except those who live in the immediate neighborhood. Drivers are hired and trained by the companies, but behavioral problems on the bus (as perceived and reported by the drivers) become the responsibility of the school. All students attend an assembly on bus safety presented jointly by building administrators and a bus-company representative each fall, so they are presented with guidelines for appropriate behavior early in the school year. Their parents receive a similar message at the annual fall open house. Unfortunately, student behavior does not always reflect an understanding of behavioral expectations, and parent response to disciplinary action is not always supportive.

Questions:

1. Are the district's transportation needs best met through contracted services such as these? What alternatives exist?
2. Are the responsibilities for driver training and student discipline appropriately placed?
3. Who are the shareholders in this situation and what responsibilities might they reasonably be expected to assume?
4. What lines of communication need to be opened or strengthened?

5. What procedures should be established with the students regarding bus discipline in order to avoid on-going "crisis management"?

References:

Curtis, V.B., and S.H. Smith. 1994. Taking charge of the discipline conference. *Principal* 74:39, 41, 43.

George, K.L. 1995. Fuss on the bus. *American School Board Journal* 182:33-37.

Neatrour, P.E. 1994. Riding by the rules: A practical approach to bus discipline. *Schools in the Middle* 4:25-27.

Pinsone, A.V. 1993. Monitoring for safety: District implements bus monitor program. *School Business Affairs* 59:22-23.

Schantl, W. 1991. A bus behavior modification plan for grades K-5. A practicum report. ED335787.

31. STUDENTS DRINKING ON FIELD TRIP

Problem:

As principal, you have just been presented with a lunch box and thermos by Mr. Carpenter, a fourth-grade teacher. He is very upset and explains to you that he just took it away from three boys. The thermos contains beer.

Background:

It is the middle of May. The fourth-grade class was on a field trip to a museum. On the return trip the teacher saw three students huddled over a thermos. As the students handed the thermos to him, he realized it contained beer. The principal calls the boys' parents to school immediately. The mother of Joe Brown, the boy who brought the beer, is annoyed that her son should be reprimanded (kids will be kids). The mother of Tom Green is very upset and most cooperative. The mother of Sam Black is upset. She thinks her son has been framed and is annoyed with the school. The other students of the fourth-grade class are taking sides on the issue. Some believe Sam Black was framed. The boys have gained newfound popularity among many of their peers due to their notoriety.

Questions:

1. What action would you take with the three boys?
2. How would you handle the three mothers?
3. How would you deal with the other fourth-grade students?
4. What kind of policy implications does this incident have?
5. What steps will you take to prevent this problem from occurring again?

References:

Agnello-Linden, M.F. 1992. Alcohol use and abuse in a rural school. ED341001.

Burrell, L.F. 1992. Student perceptions of alcohol consumption. *Journal of Alcohol and Drug Education* 37:107-113.

Howell, J.F. 1995. Drug and alcohol use survey results: 1990-1995. ED383796.

Schwartzkopf, L. 1994. Developing a substance abuse prevention program for at-risk elementary school students. ED377435.

Tillman, P.S. 1992. Adolescent alcoholism. January 1986 though April 1992. Current bibliographies in medicine. ED355462.

32. STUDENT STEALING

Problem:

Carol Shields, a fourth-grade student, came to the office after lunch, crying bitterly. She reported that a small terrarium that she had brought to school to show her teacher and classmates had disappeared from her desk while the class was at recess. Mrs. Swinton, the teacher, questioned the other students in the class but no one admitted to knowing the whereabouts of the terrarium.

While the class was at physical education, Mrs. Swinton decided to conduct a search of the classroom and found the terrarium hidden in Betty Mott's desk. She then informed you, the principal, of what had happened.

Background:

Carol Shields comes from a very wealthy family, is an only child, and wears very expensive clothing to school. She frequently brings expensive things to school, often brags about her exotic vacation trips, and generally flaunts her wealth.

Betty Mott lives with her third-grade sister and her mother in a substandard bungalow. Her father deserted the family two years ago. The mother is very concerned about the behavior of both of her daughters. Mrs. Mott has been known to mete out unusually harsh punishment and has spanked the girls severely for minor infractions in the past. Betty has been sent to the office several times this year for assorted disciplinary reasons. According to their teacher, Betty and Carol do not get along and have gotten into several arguments.

Questions:

1. What action would you take with Betty for stealing Carol's terrarium?
2. Is this a severe case of theft?
3. How do you get children such as Carol to modify their behavior so that others don't feel inferior?
4. Would you involve the parents of either girl?

References:

Aldridge, J.S., and J.A. Wooley. 1990. Legal guidelines for permissible student searches in the public schools. ED337895.

Franco, S.L. 1994. Adopting a policy to protect students and the school: Searches and seizures. *Quill and Scroll* 68:21.

Kadel, S. et al. 1995. Reducing school violence: Building a framework for school safety. ED391227.

Rossow, L.F., and J.A. Hininger. 1991. Students and the law. Fastback Series No. 317. ED332373.

33. SUBSTITUTE TEACHER'S FAILURE TO FOLLOW DISMISSAL PROCEDURES

Problem:

While you were at a meeting at the State Education Department today, John, a fifth grader, missed the bus at dismissal because a substitute teacher was detaining him for disciplinary reasons. John was still at school in your secretary's office when you returned at 4:30 p.m.

Background:

The secretary was unable to locate either parent, since the father was out of town on business and the mother had recently changed jobs and had not notified the school as to her new work number. John's babysitter did not have a car.

Questions:

1. How will you handle the problem of transporting John home?
2. What will you tell his parents?
3. What actions will you take with the substitute teacher?
4. Are there any actions you need to take to prevent this type of incident from happening in the future?

References:

Buchberg, W. et al. 1995. Teachers' help-one-another club. Management advice for substitutes. *Instructor* 7:12.

Cotton, D.J. 1995. Liability of educators for the negligence of others (substitutes, aides, student teachers, and new teachers). *Physical Educators* 52:70-77.

Lovley, S. 1994. A practical guide to substituting at different grade levels. *Teaching PreK-8.* 25:70-71.

Nidds, J.A., and J. McGerald. 1994. Substitute teachers: Seeking meaningful instruction in the teacher's absence. *Clearing House* 68:25-26.

Nudel, M. 1993. The schedule dilemma. *American School Board Journal* 180:37-40.

34. TEACHER ALCOHOLISM AND POOR PERFORMANCE

Problem:

Mr. Allen teaches a fifth-grade special-education class. He has difficulties managing his students, and they often cause disruptions, both in the classroom and the hallways. He has a full- time aide in the class, who plans and manages most of the individualized instruction. Parents are complaining that there is little education taking place and that the classroom lacks structure. Fellow special-education teachers are complaining that Mr. Allen participates little in curriculum planning, ordering, and other departmental functions. Both the special-education supervisor and you, the principal, have spent time in Mr.

Allen's classroom, observing and making concrete suggestions for improvement. It is common knowledge in the building that Mr. Allen has a drinking problem. Mr. Allen has discussed this problem with several staff members and has spent at least one summer vacation in a program attempting to control his addiction. He is also deeply in debt and fearful of losing his income.

Background:

Mr. Allen was not recommended for tenure by the special-education supervisor, but was recommended for tenure by the prior school principal. Mr. Allen grieved the supervisor's evaluation through the union, citing prejudice. He also questioned the authority of the supervisor to evaluate teachers, as he was a part-time employee of the district. Mr. Allen contacted the Civil Liberties Union, and subsequently the first-year supervisor withdrew his negative evaluation and Mr. Allen was granted tenure. His evaluations in the past four years continued to be satisfactory in the opinion of the principal, but only fair in the opinion of the special education supervisor, who became a full-time employee of the district.

You have recently been hired as the new principal of the elementary school, and you are in agreement with the supervisor concerning Mr. Allen's teaching performance. There is a great deal of pressure from district administration, as well as parents and teachers, to take the necessary actions to remove Mr. Allen from the classroom.

Questions:

1. List the critical problems in this case study.
2. What information do you need to make a decision regarding what to do about Mr. Allen's drinking problem?
3. Should you take action to terminate Mr. Allen? How will you proceed?
4. What will you say to Mr. Allen?

References:

Cross, B.E. 1993. How do we prepare teachers to improve race relations? *Educational Leadership* 50:64-65.

Dennis, B.L. 1990. What to do when a bad teacher doesn't get better. *Executive Educator* 12:15-16.

Pate, G.S. 1995. Prejudice reduction and the findings of research. ED383803.

35. TEACHER ARRESTED

Problem:

Ms. Prentis is a first-grade teacher at Borden Elementary School. She has twelve years of teaching experience and is respected as a good teacher, although she is considered flighty. Ms. Prentis has had a multitude of personal problems this year as she is the object of attention of two male suitors. The two men continually call her at school and even visit her during her breaks. Several times Ms. Prentis has left school on her lunch break to have lunch with one of her suitors. Some teachers have complained that she has asked them to watch her class while she answers one of her "important" phone calls. The whole situation culminated in a weekend blow-up where Ms. Prentis and her two friends were arrested after a late-night brawl. The Monday morning radio report was, "Teacher arrested in Saturday-night fracas." She was charged with obstructing justice. A copy of the newspaper report of the incident was mailed to the superintendent with a letter signed by several parents asking for her dismissal.

Background:

You are a first-year probationary principal. Ms. Prentis has worked at Borden for the full twelve years of her tenure. She is one of two first-grade teachers in the building and the one most requested by parents. The faculty has grumbled somewhat about Ms. Prentis' actions; however, in general she is well liked and respected as a teacher. There have been no formal complaints about her actions, and she has always had good evaluations by the previous principal. The rumors are that Ms. Prentis always had different boyfriends visiting her at school, but not as often as they do now. Apparently the now-retired principal chose to ignore the situation in the past.

Questions:

1. How will you address Ms. Prentis regarding the present problem, which may harm the school's image, as well as the ongoing problem regarding her personal use of school time?
2. Whom will you consult regarding this problem?
3. How will you handle the inevitable questions from the press?

4. What actions will you take with the parents of her students?

References:

DeMitchell, T.A. 1993. Private lives: Community control vs. professional autonomy. *West's Education Law Quarterly* 2:217-226.
Hooker, C.P. 1994. Terminating teachers and revoking their licensure for conduct beyond the schoolhouse gate. ED379754.
Larson, W.A., ed. 1994. When crisis strikes on campus. ED380039.
Thorpe, R.E. 1995. The first year as principal. Real-world stories from America's principals. ED394213.

36. TEACHER BELITTLING STUDENT PUBLICLY

Problem:

Mr. Smith, a sixth-grade teacher, has been transferred to three of the five elementary schools in the district during the past ten years. He has very poor classroom control. His teaching methods are very weak and antiquated. He has a great deal of difficulty with remedial students. He consistently arranges the students in rows according to ability levels. His students complain about him constantly. They accuse him of embarrassing them regularly by belittling their abilities publicly. Mr. Smith has been in this particular elementary school for five years. For the past four years he has been forced to team with two other teachers because of all the complaints against him in his first year there. In the past two years, over 80 percent of the fifth graders' parents have requested that their child not be placed in his room the next year. Of late, he has developed a nasal condition that requires him to blow his nose constantly. The children now complain he makes them sick. Parents who have had children in his class frequently state, "This year was an absolute waste for my child."

Background:

Mr. Smith has taught for approximately twenty years. He is a good-natured man and gets along well with the staff. However, he tends to keep to himself. He plans for his lessons and routinely stays after school to correct papers. You are the new principal this year and must deal with Mr. Smith.

Questions:

1. Make a list of Mr. Smith's problems. List the most serious first, the next most serious problem second, and so on.
2. What documentation should you have on Mr. Smith?
3. What can you do to assist him in improving his behavior?
4. What responses do you make regarding parents' requests?

References:

Experienced teachers handbook. First Edition. 1993. ED380459.

Niebrand, C. et al. 1992. The pocket mentor: A handbook for teachers. ED374107.

Schwartz, D. 1990. A remedy for student boredom: Stimulation through simulation. *Social Studies Review* 29:79-85.

37. TEACHER'S INABILITY TO COPE WITH STUDENTS

Problem:

Mrs. Vernon, a first-grade teacher, returned to work this year after a two-year child-rearing leave. Her second-grade class consists of 25 students, 10 of whom have serious learning and/or behavioral problems. As the year progressed, Mrs. Vernon has become less and less able to cope with the class. After three months, eight students were moved into other classes in an effort to create a more manageable situation. For a while, the situation improved in Mrs. Vernon's class.

As spring approached, Mrs. Vernon again began having trouble handling her class. Many complaints about her constant berating and screaming at her children were made to you, the principal. On two occasions she asked, and was given permission, to leave at lunchtime because she was too unstable to continue working. Her methods of asking for help consisted of terse notes to you demanding instant solutions to daily classroom management problems.

Background:

Mrs. Vernon has made it known that she returned to school with great misgivings and would rather be at home with her two children. Her unstable condition is of great concern to you and the teachers. This year several parents have already made formal requests not to have their child assigned to Mrs. Vernon's class for next year.

Questions:

1. What could you do to facilitate Mrs. Vernon's ability to better cope with her class?
2. At what point, if any, should her fellow teachers get involved in actively trying to resolve this problem?
3. What should be done if Mrs. Vernon's instability continues next year?

References:

Emmer, E.T. 1994. Towards an understanding of the primacy of classroom management and discipline. *Teaching Education* 6:65-69.

Evertson, C.M. et al. 1994. Classroom management for elementary teachers. Third edition. ED369782.

Mathur, S.R. et al. 1996. Teacher-mediated behavior management strategies for children with emotional/behavioral disorders. ED391306.

Rockwell, S. 1993. Tough to reach, tough to teach: Students with behavior problems. ED355672.

Smith, D.D., and D.P. Rivera. 1995. Discipline in special education and regular education settings. *Focus on Exceptional Children* 27:1-14.

38. TEACHER PERSONALITY

Problem:

Mrs. Burton is teaching third grade this year. Last summer eight parents called to protest their children's placement in her class. Five of the objections focused on her reputation as a "screamer" and as an irritable teacher. Three parents who have had other children assigned to her class expressed concern over the fact that Mrs. Burton provides little enrichment or individualization for her students.

You became principal at the beginning of this school year. During the first weeks of school, several children in Mrs. Burton's class complained of physical ailments and parents complained about having to force their children to attend school each morning. On several occasions, upon entering Mrs. Burton's classroom, you witnessed her severely reprimanding the entire class or one child. Mrs. Burton has difficulty following school routines. She is five to ten minutes late to school at least half of the time. She has left the class unattended twice for emergency health problems. (She is very overweight and often appears ill.)

Background:

After being laid off four years ago, Mrs. Burton was recalled and moved to a different grade level each year. During the year she was away from school, she took courses in computer education. She keeps a computer in her classroom and has begun to teach a few children the basic elements of programming. Mrs. Burton is well liked by her peers and is warm and sympathetic with them, although she resists any attempts by them to involve her in team-teaching activities.

Questions:

1. List Mrs. Burton's areas of weakness.
2. Develop a remediation/assistance plan for Mrs. Burton.
3. How will you deal with the parents' current complaints?
4. What are the pros and cons of honoring parent requests and transferring students out of a teacher's class? What happens when a principal honors some of these requests and not others?

References:

Baldwin, B. et al. 1990. Personality factors of elementary and secondary pre-service teachers. ED326522.

Martin, N.K. et al. 1995. Beliefs regarding classroom management style: Relationships to particular teacher personality characteristics. ED387461.

Thompson, T.C. 1992. De-programming our responses: The effects of personality on teacher responses. ED353577.

39. TEACHER PLACEMENT AFTER LEAVE

Problem:

Mr. Smith is returning to teaching after a leave of absence granted by the district, and he wishes to return to the school and grade that he left a year ago. In his absence, however, an outstanding probationary teacher has filled his position. A permanent substitute from another school has terminated her employment, and this position, in a different building and grade, has been given to Mr. Smith. Mr. Smith has many friends at his old school, has made plans for carpooling, and was looking forward to returning to the situation he knew and liked. He resents strongly being put into a different school with a different teaching assignment, and feels that he has been treated shabbily by the district and even by the union. As principal, you may recommend his placement in either school. If your reasons are sound for this placement, your suggestion will probably be followed.

Background:

You are anxious to keep the probationary teacher who replaced Mr. Smith. She is a conscientious and concerned teacher and is doing innovative projects in her classroom. She feels badly about "stealing" Mr. Smith's position, and her discomfort has been increased by the voiced disapproval of some of her colleagues, most of whom like Mr. Smith. She has offered to request a transfer to the other position in order to allow Mr. Smith to return to his old job. He has been successful with the grade he previously taught, and questions his ability to succeed at the newly assigned level.

Questions:

1. What principles should guide you in your decision?
2. Where would you recommend that Mr. Smith be placed? Why?
3. How would you justify the placement and how would you communicate with the people involved?
4. What/who do you need to consult (e.g., union contract, board contract, etc.)?

References:

Beaudin, B.Q. 1993. Teachers who interrupt their careers: Characteristics of those who return to the classroom. 1993. *Educational Evaluation and Policy Analysis* 15:51-64.

Burns, R.B., and D.A. Mason. 1995. Organizational constraints on the formation of elementary school classes. *American Journal of Education* 103:185-212.

Educator Reserve Pool Study. 1992. ED353256.

Pflaum, S.W., and T. Abramson. 1990. Teacher assignment, hiring, and preparation: Minority teachers in New York City. *Urban Review* 22:17-31.

40. TEACHER SEXUAL MISCONDUCT

Problem:

It is two weeks before the end of your second year as principal at Newmark Elementary School. On Friday, Jonathan Williams' mother, a teacher at the high school, informed you, the principal, that she has been unable to make Jonathan go to school for the past three days even though he was not ill. After much persuasion, Jonathan finally told his mother about a problem he had last week when he had come in early to receive extra help in math from Mr. Nicholson, his fifth-grade teacher. While Jonathan was standing at the teacher's desk, Mr. Nicholson placed his arm around Jonathan's waist and put his hand down inside the front of his pants. After this incident became known this week, three other boys have come forward with the same type of stories about Mr. Nicholson.

Background:

Mr. Nicholson is a married man of forty-five who has taught in the school system for eleven years. He rents a house in the school district and has a permanent residence 200 miles away, where his wife resides. He has been accused by some students of having favorites in the class who are always boys. Mr. Nicholson is well liked by the staff and this incident has been a great shock to the teachers and the friends who knew him. Mr. Nicholson has not denied the allegation.

Questions:

1. How will you determine whether these accusations are true?
2. What actions will you take with Mr. Nicholson?
3. How will you deal with the boys who are making the accusations?
4. What will you say to the parents of the students who are involved?
5. What are the ethical and legal implications of this case?

References:

Fossey, R., and T. DeMitchell. 1995. "Let the master respond": Should schools be strictly liable when employees sexually abuse children? ED386829.

Lane, F., Jr. 1995. Sexual misconduct of school employees: Supervisory school officials' liability under Section 1983. *School Law Bulletin* 26:9-16.

Mawdsley, R.D., and F.M. Hampton. 1992. Sexual misconduct by school employees involving students. *West's Education Law Quarterly* 1:284-295.

Regotti, T.L. 1992. Negligent hiring and retaining of sexually abusive teachers. *West's Education Law Quarterly* 1:254-261.

Stein, N. 1993. Secrets in full view: Sexual harassment in our K-12 schools. ED371264.

41. TEACHER/TEACHER AFFAIR

Problem:

Recently, rumors have been floating around about Mr. Kelly and Ms. Johnson. Fifth grade students are telling stories about how "close" Mr. Kelly and Ms. Johnson are. The two are inseparable and have been seen together everywhere, in and out of school. They both arrive at work and leave at the same time. There are times during the day when the two of them have been found together behind closed doors. Mr. Kelly is a married man and his wife works in another school in the same district. Parents have called you, the principal, complaining about this relationship and want to know what you plan to do about their "affair."

Background:

Mr. Kelly and Ms. Johnson have been instructing the only two fifth-grade classes in Mountain View Elementary School for over ten years. Throughout this time they have shared materials, classroom space, planning time, and field trips. Their fifth-grade students have always done well academically and socially. The fifth-grade program has earned a wonderful reputation as parents are very pleased with their children's progress.

Questions:

1. How will you determine what is really happening between these two teachers?
2. What actions will you take with Mr. Kelly and Ms. Johnson?
3. How will you respond to the parents' complaints?
4. Should you break up the fifth-grade program?

5. How will you neutralize the rumors and the negative public relations arising out of this situation?

References:

Cole, A.L. 1991. Relationships in the workplace: Doing what comes naturally? ED333001.
Crone, L.J., and C. Teddlie. 1995. Further examination of teacher behavior in differentially effective schools: Selection and socialization process. *Journal of Classroom Interaction* 30:1-9.
Staton, A.Q., and S.L. Hunt. 1992. Teacher socialization: Review and conceptualization. *Communication Education* 41:109-137.

42. TEAM-TEACHING CONFLICT

Problem:

Miss Green and Mrs. Knight are teachers in the prekindergarten program and are supposed to work together as a team. Mrs. Knight has complained that Miss Green does not listen to anything she says. Miss Green apparently has no respect for Mrs. Knight and shows it. In addition, a parent told you, the principal, that she was offended by Mrs. Knight's straightforward manner. Another parent said that her child cried whenever Mrs. Knight came near the child. Other staff have told you that Mrs. Knight is difficult to get along with.

Background:

Mrs. Knight is considerably older than Miss Green and has a very strong personality. Both teachers started working in different classes, but due to staff changes, they both ended up in the prekindergarten program. Miss Green doesn't appear very willing to soften her attitude toward Mrs. Knight, even after you have encouraged her to do so. Mrs. Knight wants to please others but does not see herself the way others see her. She feels that if she tries to change in order to get along, she will no longer be herself. Reassignment is not an option at this time.

Questions:

1. How should the immediate situation be resolved?
2. How should parents' concerns about Mrs. Knight be addressed?

3. How can teamwork and mutual respect be facilitated between these two teachers?
4. What is the best solution for the staff, parents, and the children?

References:

Elkind, D. 1996. Early childhood education: What should we expect? *Principal* 75:11-13.

Kostelnik, M.J. 1992. A guide to team teaching in early childhood education. ED358909.

Lopez, M.E., and T. Schultz. 1996. Serving young children: Strategies for success. *Principal* 75:21-24.

Sheerer, M.A., and K.L. Bauer. 1996. Models of supervision in early childhood programs: Implications for training. *Early Childhood Education Journal* 23:201-206.

Thornton, J.R. 1990. Food for thought. Team teaching: A relationship based on trust and communication. *Young Children* 45:40-43.

43. TERMINATION OF NEW TEACHER

Problem:

Ms. Roberts, a new hire to the school in September, has been absent for six weeks because of an operation. Sick days are on an earn-as-you-go basis; prior to the operation, she had used 33 days. Consequently the central board has officially terminated her appointment. She was also tardy 15 days. Reference checks made since she was hired reveal that her teaching credentials appear not to be in order. Ms. Roberts maintains that she had submitted the necessary papers and that it must be a computer error. She has contacted you, the principal, several times requesting that she come back to work. She states that she feels wonderful and has a clean bill of health from her doctor. Another teacher in the school gave birth prematurely, creating an opportunity to reinstate Ms. Roberts. This vacancy must be filled quickly, since substitutes are not readily available.

Background:

Ms. Roberts taught a combined kindergarten grade class. Her previous experience was in day care and in elementary grades as a day-to-day substitute. Although her classroom often seemed chaotic and somewhat weak academically, she established a warm, positive relationship with the difficult children in her room. She is respected and well liked by the other members of the staff. Early in the year Ms. Robert's mother died of uterine cancer. Some months later she herself was found to have a tumor. Her doctor urged her to take care of it early; she underwent the operation and the tumor was benign.

Questions:

1. Should you, as principal, recommend that the district reinstate Ms. Roberts?
2. How can you ascertain whether Ms. Roberts is the victim of circumstance or whether past performance indicates a negative pattern?
3. What do you need to know about the status of her teaching credentials? How will you verify whether her credentials are in order?

References:

Fowler, D. 1995. Ten ways to control absenteeism. *Early Childhood News* 7:36-37.

Imants, J., and A. Van Zoelen. 1995. Teachers' sickness absence in primary schools, school climate and teachers' sense of efficacy. *School Organization* 15:77-86.

Peterson, S. 1991. When the teacher's away. ED336371.

CHAPTER FOUR

Middle-School and Junior-High Case Studies

By the time students reach middle school or junior high, most become quickly aware of teachers' problems. They discuss these problems among themselves and often tell their parents about incidents occurring at school that are inappropriate on the part of teachers. At a time when preadolescence is causing turmoil both physically and psychologically, students need stability among the adults in their lives, as well as nurturing, focus, direction, and respect as individuals. When teachers violate their professional code of ethics by psychologically or physically abusing students, immeasurable damage can occur to fragile student psyches, with future implications for the rest of their school years. Since teachers serve as role models for students, principals need to develop a plan for dealing with negative and unprofessional teacher behavior.

Within this section of case studies, teacher problems include refusal to accept change; lack of student control and other classroom management problems; losing students during a field trip; declining enrollment in foreign-language courses; the harm caused by gossip; a personal leave request; a student-activity accounts audit; unfair student punishment; excessive absenteeism; emotional problems; teacher alcoholism; provocative behavior with students; mistreatment of students; reassignment; teacher dismissal; seniority issues; teacher-teacher conflicts; the stalking of a teacher; failure to obey rules; work-related injuries; teaching style; and team teaching.

Parent-related case studies include a parent complaint about cooperative learning; a negative parent-teacher conference; complaints about teacher expectations; a request not to have a student placed with a specific teacher; demands made by the PTA president; and the parental role in student retention.

Student-related cases include leaving school without permission; fear of a teacher; student-to-student sexual assault; selling stolen candy; a student failing all subjects; physically threatening a teacher; and insubordination.

44. DECLINING ENROLLMENT IN FOREIGN-LANGUAGE TEACHER'S CLASS

Problem:

For the last two years, the enrollment in Mr. Nagy's foreign-language program at the middle school has been dropping. Students in his classes complain that he has a negative attitude about everything. Parents have called the principal to complain that large numbers of his students are not passing and that he simply doesn't take the time and effort to help them. He does stay after school to assist students one day per week as per contractual agreement. Recently, he had a confrontation with you, the principal, about issuing a textbook to a student who had the book stolen. The student did not pay for the book and Mr. Nagy would not issue another book even after the chairman had instructed him to do so. He claimed that the student should pay regardless of the circumstances. At this point you stepped in and told the teacher to issue the book. The teacher said he would not personally issue the book, but he would give it to you to give to the student. This is your first year as principal in that school.

Background:

Mr. Nagy is a tenured foreign-language teacher with twenty years of experience in the same district. He has done a satisfactory job in the classroom, gotten along with most of the staff, and even coached after school. However, he has a reputation of being a negative person, constantly bad-mouthing the administration and disagreeing with many administrative decisions. Presently, he doesn't coach, nor is he involved with other school activities.

Questions:

1. What should you do about the stolen book incident?

2. What steps should you take to assist Mr. Nagy to improve his attitude?
3. What effect do negative staff members have on the rest of the staff?
4. What are the implications for the foreign-language program if the enrollment in Mr. Nagy's class continues to decline?

References:

Di Donato, R. 1987. The foreign language teacher: Confronting an ever-changing profession. ED337007.

Gahala, E.M. 1986. Increasing student participation in the foreign language class. ED337001.

Kleinsasser, R.C. 1992. Foreign language teacher attrition: A look at those leaving public schools in Illinois. *Foreign Language Annals* 25:295-304.

Kottman, T. 1990. Counseling middle school students: Techniques that work. *Elementary School Guidance and Counseling* 25:138-145.

Raphael, J. 1996. New beginnings for new middle school students. *Educational Leadership* 54:56-59.

45. DEMANDS OF PTA PRESIDENT

Problem:

You have just been named principal of Hawthorne School, a K-8 building. Mrs. Henderson, the PTA president, has made an appointment to see you on your third day on the job. As she enters your office and begins to talk with you, you notice that she seems very negative. She quickly informs you that the PTA is very powerful in this district, and that this organization played a key role in getting rid of your predecessor. She then demands that you look for some expensive camera equipment that the PTA purchased for the school when the other principal was there, because the PTA suspects that he "stole" these items and took them with him to his new job upstate.

Background:

Hawthorne School is located in one of the most prestigious school districts in the state. The student population is very homogeneous. The per-capita wealth is among the highest in the state and in the nation. Parents have always been very vocal and the PTA has been very involved in the school. The last principal felt intimidated by parental and PTA pressure and capitulated to them on several issues.

Questions:

1. How do you respond to Mrs. Henderson's demands and accusations about the former principal?
2. What plan will you develop for working with the PTA and establishing parameters for their involvement?
3. Who else will you consult regarding the role of the PTA in other schools in the district?
4. How will you regain "control" of the situation?

References:

Fruchter, N. et al. 1992. New directions in parent involvement. ED360683.

Parent involvement in education. Indicator of the month. 1994. ED374923.

Radd, T.R. 1993. Restructuring parent-teacher organizations to increase parental influence on the educational process. *Elementary School Guidance and Counseling* 27:280-287.

Whitfill, K. 1994. PTA puts children first. *PTA Today* 19:4.

46. EFFECTS OF TEACHER GOSSIP

Problem:

Mrs. Devin, an eighth-grade English teacher, appears friendly and helpful, especially to new staff. She is privy to a good deal of personal information. Armed with juicy tidbits and slanted truths, Mrs. Devin has gossiped to anyone who would listen. She has begun to include the parents of students in her classes. Her behavior has caused a great deal of turmoil and anger among other teachers as well as parents in the district. You are the new principal and must deal with this problem.

Background:

Mrs. Devin is a tenured junior-high school English teacher with over ten years' experience in the district. She is a capable, creative, and effective teacher who has constantly received excellent evaluations from the former principal. During her years in the district, she has taught both advanced and basic classes with equal success. Mrs. Devin is always willing to take on additional responsibilities and duties.

Questions:

1. What action would you, as the new school principal, take with Mrs. Devin?
2. How would you deal with the anger of the school staff?
3. What steps will you take to improve the overall school climate?
4. How would you respond to the parents' concerns?

References:

Ackerman, R. et al. 1996. Case stories: Telling tales about school. *Educational Leadership* 53:21-23.

Anderson, B. 1995. The dirt on gossip. *Executive Educator* 17:14-18.

Riepe, L. 1995. Understanding and managing negativity in the workplace. *Child Care Information Exchange* 101:61-64.

Watson, C.H. 1990. Gossip and the guidance counselor: An ethical dilemma. *School Counselor* 38:34-39.

Wilson, A.P., and T.G. Bishard. 1994. Psst. Here's the dirt on gossip. *American School Board Journal* 181:27-29.

47. EXCESSIVE TEACHER ABSENTEEISM

Problem:

For the past three years, Ms. Simon, a junior-high school foreign-language teacher, has been absent excessively–usually before and after school vacations, taking both sick days and personal days. Complaints about back problems, with letters from her chiropractor, have documented her need to be absent from school. Also, during the past three years Ms. Simon was on Workmen's Compensation due to work-related injuries. She claimed that a file cabinet fell on her foot, and she injured her back moving heavy boxes in the classroom. There were no witnesses to these incidents. Other department members have complained to the principal because they have had to absorb her students into their classes when no substitute was provided. The other teachers feel that she is feigning illness and is using her accumulated days dishonestly, extending vacation and taking care of personal business.

Background:

Ms. Simon is a twenty-year veteran in the system. She is an excellent teacher, effective with students and parents, and cooperative with other teachers in the department. Her innovative and creative approach to teaching has resulted in favorable publicity in district newsletters and in grants for exemplary programs.

Questions:

1. What approach would you take with the teacher?
2. As principal, what would be said to the other department faculty members?
3. Which other district administrators should be consulted?

References:

Ehrenberg, R.G. et al. 1991. School district leave policies, teacher absenteeism, and student achievement. *Journal of Human Resources* 26:72-105.

Jacobson, S.L. 1990. Attendance incentives and teacher absenteeism. *Planning and Changing* 21:78-93.

Jacobson, S.L. et al. 1993. Toward a reconception of absence in the school workplace: Teacher absenteeism as invention and social exchange. ED357502.

Pitkiff, E. 1993. Teacher absenteeism: What administrators can do. *NASSP Bulletin* 77:39-45.

48. FAILURE TO ACCOUNT FOR STUDENTS DURING FIELD TRIP

Problem:

Mr. Morgan teaches social studies at the junior high and serves as an advisor to the student council. Each year the council plans a field trip. This year they planned to go to the United Nations and because of the holiday season, to Rockefeller Center to see the Christmas tree. After the tour of the U.N., they went to Rockefeller Center. The students were told that they could "do their own thing" and then meet back at the bus at the appointed time. They returned as directed and departed for home without realizing that they were missing two female students, who subsequently called the school in tears. About halfway home the bus driver received a radio dispatch informing him that two students were left behind in New York City. The bus continued its trip back to the school. Upon their return, you, the principal, directed Mr. Morgan to return to the city by car to get the students and to call the parents as soon as he had the children under his supervision. Mr. Morgan, however, first called his wife to inform her of the day's happenings, and this took at least half an hour. He got stuck in traffic and didn't reach the students until 6:00 p.m. He never contacted the parents but simply returned back to the school with the children at about 7:30 p.m. The parents were frantic.

Background:

Mr. Morgan has taught social studies at the junior high school for fifteen years. He is a kindhearted soul but not very organized. He has poor classroom management as exemplified by the lack of structure in his lesson plans and daily classroom activities. Furthermore, his inability to maintain adequate daily records has led to problems in assigning grades. This became apparent on more than one occasion when students' grades were questioned by their parents. The administration is not happy with his performance of late, and they have spoken with him about it. They have also put their concerns in writing and placed them into his personnel file.

Questions:

1. What is your plan for dealing with Mr. Morgan?
2. What strategies will you take in addressing the parents' concerns?
3. How will you deal with the two girls?
4. What will you do to prevent this from happening again?

References:

Beiersdorfer, R.E., and W.E. Davis. 1994. Suggestions for planning a class field trip. *Journal of College Science Teaching* 23:307-311.

Caldwell, J.R. 1994. String. *Science Activities* 31:8-10.

Close call: Marloes again. 1994. *Journal of Adventure, Education, and Outdoor Leadership* 11:4-5.

From classroom teacher to field trip leader. Hints for getting there. 1988. ED326418.

Zielinski, E. J. 1987. So you want to take a field trip. ED299079.

49. IMPROVEMENT OF CLASSROOM MANAGEMENT SKILLS

Problem:

Jim Atkins is a 50-year-old middle-school math teacher and the chairperson of the math and science departments. He has very little student control in his classes. His colleagues, teaching in the same area, have taken to closing their doors so that their classes will not be disturbed by the noise. They have complained to you, the principal, about the problem. Last year, the superintendent told you to give him one more year and then if he did not turn the situation around, initiate disciplinary proceedings.

Background:

Mr. Atkins has been in education for twenty-four years and in the district for eleven years. He began his math teaching in another district and, after five years, was appointed the district's junior-high principal for the next six years. He was then appointed as the administrative assistant to the superintendent for the next two years. Following these administrative experiences, Mr. Atkins decided, although the record is not clear why, to return to the classroom. His letter of application to your district indicated that he just felt that his talents and interests were more in the field of teaching rather than administration. Mr. Atkins has taught math in grades eight, nine, and ten, for several years and is currently an eighth-grade teacher in the middle school.

Two years ago, there were protracted contract negotiations that led to departments being amalgamated under single chairpersons. Although this role was not directly supervisory in nature, chairpersons were asked to go into classrooms for curriculum purposes. Teachers were generally discouraged "unofficially" by the union from applying for these positions. Eventually, Mr. Atkins volunteered to apply for the math/science chairperson and was the only person to do so.

Two years ago, your first year as middle-school principal, the superintendent and the assistant principal met with you to discuss the problems that Mr. Atkins was having with his classes. You observed his class several times. His style was to try and talk above the various conversations that were going on in his room and to let students walk out to go to the bathroom whenever they felt like it. You spoke with him about his classroom management at some length, but had the feeling that he really did not recognize it as a problem. After clearing it with the math teachers, you directed him to stop in and observe some of the styles and successful practices that other teachers in his department were using.

You and the assistant principal spoke with Mr. Atkins several times last year, but the situation did not improve. At your conference at the end of the school year, Mr. Atkins said that this had been a difficult year for him because of problems at home, but he chose not to expand upon that issue. He felt that he could continue to serve as chairperson and also improve his classroom situation.

This year there has been no improvement. Mr. Atkins repeatedly lost his temper and bellowed at the students in his room, despite the fact that you shared a number of articles on discipline with him, and sent him to a two-day classroom management workshop. It is now November, and, in the superintendent's words, "He must shape up or ship out."

Questions:

1. How will you develop a plan of assistance for him? Who and/or what resources should be included in this plan?
2. What documentation should you have kept last year? This year?
3. What steps will you take to initiate disciplinary proceedings against Mr. Atkins?
4. Should Mr. Atkins be allowed to continue as chairperson?

References:

Albert, L. 1990. Cooperative discipline: Classroom management that promotes self-esteem. ED328555.

Ellis, D.W., and P.J. Karr-Kidwell. 1995. A study of assertive discipline and recommendations for effective classroom management methods. ED379207.

Emmer, E.T. et al. 1994. Classroom management for secondary teachers. Third edition. ED369781.

Rancifer, J.L. 1995. The real cutting edge in education: Changing misbehaving students in the classroom and school. ED382576.

Tips for Beginners: Positive classroom management. 1992. *Mathematics Teacher* 85:720-721.

50. INTERDISCIPLINARY TEACHER TEAM

Problem:

Dr. Clark is an eighth-grade science teacher in a school that subscribes to team teaching. Dr. Clark has difficulty presenting the science curriculum to the students at their level. There is a high level of concern over her inability to control her classes. Her students' disruptive antics in the classroom often spill into the hallways. The other team teachers tend to ignore Dr. Clark's problems. The science department coordinator, who is also the assistant principal, has been spending a great deal of time on this problem. Lately, he has been spending a minimum of one hour a day in assisting this teacher in discipline, and additional time documenting the problem.

Background:

Dr. Clark has a Ph.D. in biochemistry and physics. She has brought a great deal of prestige to the school district by her involvement in local environmental ventures and scientific research. She is a tenured teacher who has taught in the school district for more than twenty years. She truly believes that all children are good and "incapable of any wrong acts." She has brought up her own children in the same way and each has gone on to great success in their fields. Although Dr. Clark has significant medical problems, her attendance record is good. Her fellow teachers are aware of these medical difficulties.

Questions:

1. Develop an assistance plan for Dr. Clark.
2. What role will the science department coordinator/assistant principal play in implementing this plan?
3. How will you deal with Dr. Clark's philosophy that "children are incapable of any wrong acts?"
4. What impact might medical problems have on a teacher's behavior and performance?

References:

Ehman, L.H. 1995. Interdisciplinary teacher teams: A first year's experience in a restructuring middle school. ED390845.

Gullatt, D.E. 1995. Effective leadership in the middle school classroom. ED388454.

Kruse, S., and K.S. Louis. 1995. Teacher teaming-opportunities and dilemmas. ED383082.

Powell, R.R., and R. Mills. 1994. Five types of mentoring build knowledge on interdisciplinary teams. *Middle School Journal* 26:24-30.

Sevick, M.J. 1989. A program to increase effective teaming in the middle school. ED324109.

51. LACK OF STUDENT CONTROL BY TEACHER

Problem:

Mrs. Jensen has requested that her teaching assignment for the next school year be with the same age group and with many of the same students she was assigned to this past year. Because of the experiences witnessed by the administration and the teaching staff, there are questions whether Mrs. Jensen would be suitable with any group of students.

Background:

Mrs. Jensen has been tenured for three years and teaches in a special-education program for emotionally disturbed youngsters. She generally taught classes of students from nine to twelve years of age, but this last year had a class of nine boys ages thirteen to fifteen. A year ago, her inability to control and manage the students resulted in such incidents as a tempera-paint fight in the room, a broken window from thrown blocks, all the hooks broken off in the coat closet, a broken table leg, and her arm jammed in the door by her students. There was constant lack of control in the hallway and at recess as well.

During this school year, with the older boys, there have been constant fights in the room. Furniture has been thrown around the room. The more powerful boys chase the smaller students down the hallway. The rest of the staff is becoming annoyed with Mrs. Jensen's students wandering around the school and disturbing their classrooms.

As the new principal this year, you met with Mrs. Jensen during the second week of school. Mrs. Jensen requested time to let her work out her problems. She abhorred violence and felt that a strong administrative figure in her classroom only made it more difficult for her to manage her students after you left. You heeded her request and informed all necessary staff to refer Mrs. Jensen's problems to Mrs. Jensen.

It is now mid-February and some staff members are asking why all other students are called to task for misbehavior, while the misdeeds of Mrs. Jensen's students are ignored.

Questions:

1. What would you do with Mrs. Jensen for the rest of this year? For next year?
2. How do you respond to faculty concerns for equitable treatment of students as well as the health and safety of their students?
3. Do you establish different behavioral standards for students with special needs?
4. Do you honor Mrs. Jensen's request?

References:

Caissy, G.A. 1994. Early adolescence: Understanding the 10 to 15 year old. ED385387.

DiGiulio, R. 1995. Positive classroom management: A step-by-step guide to successfully running the show without destroying student dignity. ED388625.

Kameenui, E.J., and C.B. Darch. 1995. Instructional classroom management: A proactive approach to behavior management. ED380431.

Martin, N.K., and B. Baldwin. 1996. Perspectives regarding classroom management style: Differences between elementary and secondary level teachers. ED393835.

52. MISTREATMENT OF STUDENTS BY A TEACHER

Problem:

In the span of two months (January and February), you, the principal of Harris Junior High School, have had three sets of parents visit you concerning the same problem. They each requested that their children be transferred from Mr. Kilinger's seventh-grade math class. In the fall, there had been various complaints about Mr. Kilinger's attitude, language, and treatment of children, but you had handled them all and thought that things had improved. The parents' complaints had a common thread: the children were performing poorly; the students were confused and did not understand what was expected of them; the parents felt their children were being berated and were victims of sarcasm; and Mr. Kilinger made inappropriate remarks and shouted at them.

You met with Mr. Kilinger and related the problems. Mr. Kilinger said he only yelled at the children to maintain order and did not yell any more than the other teachers in the building. He also stated he had been given an unruly group of children whose parents had never taught them respect. He said there was little hope for these children to succeed. He claimed they didn't understand directions, were half asleep during class, and didn't care at all about school.

Background:

Mr. Kilinger taught twelve years at the ninth-grade level in the district. This is his first year in the seventh grade. He had been moved to the lower grade level because of declining enrollment and fewer students electing high-school math courses.

Questions:

1. How should you handle the parents?
2. Will you move the students as requested?
3. What approaches might you take with Mr. Kilinger?
4. What suggestions can you make to improve this situation?

References:

Ferreira, M.M. et al. 1995. The caring culture of a suburban middle school. ED385011.

Gullatt, D.E. 1995. Effective leadership in the middle school classroom. ED388454.

Scales, P.C., and C.K. McEwin. 1994. Growing pains: The making of America's middle school teachers. ED381497.

Van Allen, L. 1995. Middle school teachers are different. *English Journal* 84:113-114.

Wiles, J., and J. Bondi. 1993. The essential middle school. Second edition. ED357486.

53. PARENT COMPLAINT ABOUT COOPERATIVE LEARNING

Problem:

Mrs. Wright, parent of a seventh-grade student, calls you to complain that cooperative learning is used extensively in her child's classes. Mrs. Wright is not happy with cooperative learning and claims that she speaks for many other dissatisfied parents. She claims that her bright child is always placed in groups with students who do nothing. This results in her child doing all the work for her group and having to teach material to her slower groupmates. Mrs. Wright says that cooperative learning is hindering her child's progress.

Background:

A number of teachers in the district have used group activities in their classes in the past and called these activities cooperative learning. These teachers often gave group grades for work and penalized all members of a group if one or more members did not complete the work. A large number of district teachers have now been trained to use the cooperative learning model, and all teachers in the building have been trained.

Questions:

1. Are teachers using cooperative learning effectively? How do you know?
2. Whom can you consult to help address the concerns of parents as well as the concerns of teachers?
3. Is the parent perception of the current situation, and of cooperative learning in general, accurate?
4. How can parents become more knowledgeable about what should and should not take place in properly applied cooperative learning situations?
5. How can teachers increase their expertise in using all methods of classroom organization?
6. Mrs. Wright's concerns might be representative of other parents' concerns about cooperative learning. As the instructional leader of the school, what can you do to educate parents about cooperative learning and other nontraditional instructional approaches?

References:

Crosby, M.G., and F.M. Owens. 1993. The disadvantages of tracking and ability grouping: A look at cooperative learning as an alternative. A series of solutions and strategies. ED358184.

Johnson, D.W. et al. 1994. Cooperative learning in the classroom. ED379263.

Roy, P., and J. Hoch. 1994. Cooperative learning: A principal's perspective. *Principal* 73:27-29.

Slavin, R.E. 1995. Cooperative learning and intergroup relations. ED382730.

Sparapani, E.F. et al. 1994. Cooperative learning: What teachers know about it and when they use it. ED367605.

54. PARENT REQUEST AGAINST PLACEMENT WITH SPECIFIC TEACHER

Problem:

Over the past two years, many parents have been voicing their concerns about Mr. Tenorel, a seventh-grade teacher in your building. Children in his class have told their parents how mean he is and that they are afraid of him. On more than one occasion, you have witnessed Mr. Tenorel reprimanding a student in a threatening manner. Other teachers in the building have reported similar experiences to you.

His class is one governed by fear, not respect. Parents often call to report that their son or daughter was forced to do a writing assignment as punishment for a supposed infraction of class rules, but the student never had the chance to explain his/her side of the story. His reputation is known throughout the community. Several parents of sixth graders began calling you in January to request that their children be placed in the other teacher's class next year. You have spoken to Mr. Tenorel about his behavior, but he seems set in his ways and doesn't feel that there is a problem.

Background:

Mr. Tenorel is a tenured teacher with over thirty years of experience. You are in your tenure year as principal and have previously spent twenty years teaching seventh grade in the same district. What makes the situation interesting is that Mr. Tenorel used to be the assistant principal in the same building where you used to teach. Thus you are now the "boss" for your one-time superior.

Mr. Tenorel is a highly confrontational man who does not take constructive criticism with an open mind. He is planning on retiring in two or three years and sees no reason to change what has worked "like a charm" for over thirty years. He believes that his class lessons are always exceptional, and he doesn't seem to care what others, especially parents, think of him.

Questions:

1. How should you deal with an ex-superior whose methods of discipline and classroom management are called into question?
2. How should you respond to parents when the parents register a complaint to you concerning the above problems?
3. What strategies can you take to relieve the fears the sixth-grade parents are having about their children being assigned to his class?

References:

Fruchter, N. et al. 1993. New directions in parent involvement. *Equity and Choice* 9:33-43.

Lynn, L. 1994. Building parent involvement. Brief to principals. ED366094.

Otterbourg, S. D. 1996. Education today parent involvement handbook. Second edition. ED396022.

Types of contact between parents and school personnel. Indicator of the month. 1996. ED395385.

Wheeler, P. 1992. Promoting parent involvement in secondary schools. *NASSP Bulletin* 76:28-35.

55. PARENT-TEACHER CONFERENCE

Problem:

Mrs. Jones came to the junior high school to see her son's teachers during the last week of November. She spoke to four of his six teachers. Each conversation was monopolized by Mrs. Jones and ended with her calling the teachers "jackasses and/or witches" and the teachers walking away from her. Mrs. Jones then approached the fifth teacher. This teacher decided to just listen. Mrs. Jones began the conversation with "So why is David doing so poorly?" The teacher was not permitted to finish three words when Mrs. Jones interrupted to give her philosophy on education and classroom management.

Approximately one hour after the school day ended, you, the principal, received a call from the superintendent. Mrs. Jones has gone there and complained about how the school was being run.

Background:

This parent is the mother of six children, four of whom have already gone through the elementary and junior high schools. The sixth child is now in your program. It's general knowledge and there is general agreement that mental problems are prevalent throughout the family. The district office is aware of the disruptive nature of the children and the problems their mother causes. However, for one reason or another, they always agree to her demands and she continues to overstep the limits of a concerned and interested parent.

Questions:

1. How would you deal with Mrs. Jones?
2. What discussions will you have with the superintendent regarding a plan of action for Mrs. Jones?
3. What actions will you take to help David?

References:

Markam, R. 1995. Parent communication: Preparing for parent-teacher conferences. ED378626.

McCarty, H. 1994. Ten keys to successful parent involvement and parent conferencing. ED372866.

Potter, L. 1996. How to improve parent-teacher conferences: A guide for parents from the principal. Tips for parents from NASSP. ED393198.

Seldin, C.A. 1991. Parent/teacher conferencing: A three-year study to enrich communication. ED338597.

Shaughnessy, M.F. 1991. The parent-teacher conference. ED355021.

56. PARENTAL COMPLAINTS ABOUT TEACHER EXPECTATIONS

Problem:

Mrs. Swanson has been working on a pilot math curriculum for almost two years. She has spent days writing proposals and attending numerous workshops, and has shown a great effort in coordinating special field trips, culminating activities, and in-depth student projects for the program. Several parents, however, are indignant about her high-handed manner with the students. They feel her expectations of their children and the workload is too high for junior high school. They also complain that she is cold and inflexible in her personal relations with the children and with them. The complaints, in the form of letters, phone calls, and school visits, have come to you, the new junior-high school principal. You meet with Mrs. Swanson and her department chairman to discuss these complaints. You also inform her that the future of the pilot curriculum is in jeopardy if parents keep complaining about her behavior.

Background:

Mrs. Swanson has been a controversial figure for many years. Some students despise her, some admire her, and all will remember her as a stern disciplinarian and a master teacher. Her admirers have written letters of praise and have spoken highly of her. Her critics have been equally vocal, requesting that their children be taken out of her class because of personality conflicts or a laxity on Mrs. Swanson's part in returning calls and communicating problems to the parents. She and her department chairman do not get along very well. This pilot study was the first curriculum work Mrs. Swanson had initiated in years. She was shattered after the meeting with you and the department chairman.

Questions:

1. How would you handle Mrs. Swanson's public relations with the parents?
2. How would you handle Mrs. Swanson's classroom manner?
3. How would you handle Mrs. Swanson's relationship with the department chairman?
4. How would you handle Mrs. Swanson's feelings after the summit meeting?
5. What will you do to salvage the pilot math curriculum?

References:

Albert, L. 1995. Discipline. Is it a dirty word? *Learning* 24:43-46.
Bamburg, J.D. 1994. Raising expectations to improve student learning. Urban monograph series. ED378290.

Kohn, A. 1995. Discipline is the problem-not the solution. *Learning* 24:34.

Matthews, K.M. and others. 1993. Helping teachers motivate students: Sixteen case studies (with reports on 34 other studies in process). ED354604.

Spickelmier, D. et al. 1995. Use positive discipline for middle school students. *Strategies* 8:5-8.

57. PARENTAL ROLE IN STUDENT RETENTION

Problem:

Patti Keyes is in the sixth grade. In January, the teacher held a parent conference to discuss retention. Patti's mother wanted only to discuss her current work and her outside activities. When the subject of retention was brought up, Mrs. Keyes avoided the subject. When the teacher persisted, the mother said she had another appointment and left. The teacher scheduled a second conference and requested that both Mr. and Mrs. Keyes attend. The subject of retention was the only subject discussed at this conference. The parents left without giving any indication of whether they agreed or disagreed with the teacher; you, the new principal, the school psychologist, and a reading specialist were also present at this conference. The psychologist and reading specialist had seen Patti before and agreed that she should be retained. After two more conferences, it came out that if Patti was retained it would be a very difficult stigma for the family to bear, especially the grandparents. Mrs. Keyes left angry after each conference and is threatening to go to the board of education if Patti is retained.

Background:

After checking with Patti's past teachers, you discovered that retention had been discussed at least twice, but after the conferences with Mrs. Keyes, no one pursued it. Mrs. Keyes had recently received her B.S. degree and was working on her master's degree in reading. She felt over the summer that she could bring Patti to where she needed to be for the seventh grade.

Questions:

1. Is retention a wise instructional decision for this student?
2. What other remediation, testing, etc., should occur before retention is recommended?

3. Should an individual teacher have the right to recommend that a student be retained?
4. Do parents have the right to refuse retention for their child?
5. How will you handle these parents who seem to have taken control over Patti's placement over the years?

References:

Foster, J.E. 1993. Reviews of Research: Retaining children in grade. *Childhood Education* 70:38-43.
Harvey, B.H. 1994. To retain or not? There is no question. ED369177.
Natale, J.A. 1991. Promotion or retention? Ideas are changing–again. *Executive Educator* 13:15-18.
Stencich, J. 1994. The impact of early grade retention on the academic achievement and self-esteem of seventh and eight grade students. ED393026.
Stephen, V.P. 1992. Alternatives to retention: Practical strategies for teachers. *Critical Issues in Teacher Education* 2:1-7.

58. REQUEST FOR PERSONAL LEAVE DAY

Problem:

Mr. Jones, a middle-school math teacher and junior varsity baseball coach at the high school, requested a paid conference day through the school-district athletic director to attend a baseball clinic in another state on a Friday. The athletic director neither confirmed nor denied the conference day. On the day before the clinic was to be held, Mr. Jones submitted a request for personal leave to you, the building principal, citing education reasons, since attending the clinic would enhance his skills as a baseball coach.

After conferring with the superintendent, you denied the request for leave, telling Mr. Jones that the request was submitted too late for him to find a substitute. Mr. Jones reported to school on Friday and asked for a meeting with you and the athletic director. Initially, he stated that the contract does not specifically address lead time for personal leave requests, nor should there be a problem finding a substitute, since people call in sick every morning and a substitute has always been found. In addition, he wanted to know why the athletic director did not act on his original request. After the meeting, Mr. Jones decided to grieve the denial.

Background:

Mr. Jones is a tenured math teacher in the district. For years, he has coached the junior varsity baseball team and expects to become coach of the high-school varsity when the present coach retires. Mr. Jones, however, is not too well liked by the athletic director or the superintendent. Although he has produced several winning teams, he has the reputation of being very critical of and hard-nosed with his players. Some students will not play for him when they are cut from the varsity squad. The superintendent and athletic director do not want Mr. Jones to assume the head-coach position when it becomes available.

Questions:

1. How would you as building principal address Mr. Jones' complaint?
2. How do you think the superintendent will handle the grievance when it arrives on his desk?
3. How do you think this incident will affect Mr. Jones' relationship with you and his relationship with the athletic director?
4. What policies/procedures can you put in place to alleviate this type of situation in the future?

References:

Nelson, F. H. 1994. Conditions of employment for teachers in the United States. *Clearing House* 68:82-89.

Richards, M. 1993. A good day out? Conferences and learning. *Adults Learning* 4:251-252.

Solberg, E., and T. Laughlin. 1995. The gender pay gap, fringe benefits, and occupational crowding. *Industrial and Labor Relations Review* 48:692-708.

VanZandt, C.E., and P.J. Anderson. 1992. Making the most of professional conferences: Beyond sweaty palms and boring meetings. *School Counselor* 39:263-267.

59. SCIENCE TEACHERS' REFUSAL TO ACCEPT CHANGE

Problem:

At a science department meeting that only half the department attended, the principal's plan for change was presented by Mr. Gee, the chairman. Generally, the changes were accepted by those who attended the meeting, with a few reservations and suggestions to be added. Mr. Gee accurately reported in writing the problems with the plan to the principal. The principal then wrote a report to you, the assistant superintendent for instruction, stating complete support of the staff. He omitted mentioning that half of the staff members were not represented nor were any of the department reservations or suggestions included in the report. The department became outraged and refused to support the plan.

Background:

This year Mr. Wilson, principal of North Junior High School, has a performance objective of updating the school's science program. He is an innovative principal who has had many successes implementing programs in other academic areas. Many of his ideas deal with issues such as open space, block scheduling, individual progress, elective programs, cross-grading, and thematic approaches. In past years, the science department has tried a variety of exciting approaches, methods, and organizational patterns on their own. The seven-member department consists of six teachers that have twenty or more years teaching experience and one who has been teaching two years. The members of the department are willing to make some changes; however they are concerned that one course not be eliminated from the secondary curriculum; that the changes fit into a continuum of science from elementary through high school, and that changes coincide with the new state plan that will be coming out in several months. Mr. Wilson held several unproductive meetings with the science-department members earlier in the year, and therefore decided to step back and let the department chairman take the leadership role to produce the changes. Mr. Gee has been science chairman for six years and has done an admirable job, especially regarding ordering, budget, reports, and general organization work. He follows a conventional method of communication: finding out what the principal wants, meeting regularly with the department members, and putting everything in writing through memos and minutes to keep all informed of the continuing progress.

Questions:

1. As assistant superintendent, what will be your course of action with Mr. Wilson?
2. What, if any, actions will you take with Mr. Gee?
3. What should be the principal's course of action with Mr. Gee? The science teachers'?
4. How can this type of situation be avoided in the future?

References:

Hannay, L.M., and M. Denby. 1994. Secondary school change: The role of department heads. ED380877.

Mendez-Morse, S. 1992. Leadership characteristics that facilitate school change. ED370215.

Mullen, B. et al. 1994. Collaborative leadership for promoting effective school change. *NASSP Practitioner.* ED376589.

Sashkin, M., and J. Egermeier. 1993. School change models and processes: A review and synthesis of research and practice. ED362960.

Tye, K. 1994. The goal orientation of the principal: A key factor in the success or failure of school change. ED370244.

60. STUDENT-ACTIVITY ACCOUNTS AUDIT

Problem:

At the end of this school year, the student-activity accounts were audited. One of Mr. Gray's accounts did not balance. It was found that the account was kept incorrectly. There were some incoming amounts and outgoing amounts that were not recorded. The account showed a huge debt. Mr. Gray was approached to verify the information the auditor found. Mr. Gray tried to explain that any profit was used to offset the debts created by other activity accounts.

Background:

Mr. Gray is a veteran teacher in the middle school, responsible for teaching eighth-grade social studies. For many years Mr. Gray has been involved with extracurricular activities. He is the eighth-grade advisor, student-government advisor, and the yearbook advisor. He runs practically all the student activities in the school. Mr. Gray is very popular with the students because he "runs" all the activities. He is also very popular with some of the staff who appreciate his extracurricular involvement. There are rumors that Mr. Gray is not a competent teacher, and that his extracurricular activities interfere with his teaching responsibilities.

Questions:

1. Why was Mr. Gray allowed to advise more than one extracurricular activity at the same time?
2. Why didn't the district treasurer check the accounts more frequently?
3. Was Mr. Gray the only one to sign contracts and outgoing checks?
4. What should be the principal's responsibility in supervising activity accounts?
5. As the new principal, what type of system will you develop so that this doesn't happen again?

References:

Cuzzetto, C. 1993. Internal auditing for school districts. ED364982.
Cuzzetto, C. 1995. Student activity funds: Creating a system of controls that work. *School Business Affairs* 61:18-20, 22.
DiCello, J. 1995. Decentralization calls for internal audits. *School Business Affairs* 61:16-17.

61. STUDENT FAILING ALL SUBJECTS

Problem:

Jason is a ninth-grade student in a middle school (grades 6-9). He is bright (above 130 on two I.Q. group tests), good-looking, and energetic. He has been associating with three or four male students who are considered "bad influences" by school faculty, parents, and peers. Jason has just received his report card and failed all subjects. He also has a lack of respect for any person in an authoritative role (teacher, administrator, aide, and parents). The parents have just come into school to have a conference with you, the principal. They ask, "What can we do? We can't think of anything to help Jason. Please help us!"

Background:

Mr. and Mrs. Lawrence have been divorced for over five years. They live within a quarter mile of each other. Jason has been living with his father for the past year. His other siblings (one brother and one sister) live with their mother. Mr. Lawrence owns a construction company and is away on business trips often. These usually take from three to five days at a time. When this occurs, Jason either stays with his mother or with one of his father's male friends. Mr. Lawrence stated that Jason does not and will not listen to what he asks and requests him to do. He stated that Jason continually defies him. He also mentions that just yesterday he had to resort to hitting Jason in the mouth in order to "gain back respect" that he has lost over the past few years. Jason has told you in the past that when he turns sixteen, he is going to quit school and begin a career in construction or trucking, and that he will eventually own his own company.

Questions:

1. What, if any, other school personnel would you include in this conference?
2. What options would you suggest to the parents to try to alleviate this negative attitude, as well as to try to keep Jason in school?
3. What actions will you take to help Jason?

References:

Cheney, D., and H.S. Muscott. 1996. Preventing school failure for students with emotional and behavioral disabilities through responsible inclusion. *Preventing School Failure* 40:109-116.

Pantleo, S.J. 1992. Program to reduce failure rates of ninth grade students. ED358391.

Rieck, W.A. 1994. Student failure rate: A different perspective on the problem. *NASSP Bulletin* 78:69-73.

Simons, R.L. et al. 1994. Harsh corporal punishment versus quality of parental involvement as an explanation of adolescent maladjustment. *Journal of Marriage and the Family* 56:591-607.

Waxman, H.C., and Y.N. Padron. 1995. Improving the quality of classroom instruction for students at risk of failure in urban schools. *Journal of Education* 70:44-65.

62. STUDENT FEAR OF TEACHER

Problem:

Two weeks before school ended, Dick Rogers' parents appeared at school and demanded that he be removed from Mrs. Donald's sixth-grade class. They presented a doctor's note to you stating that he was suffering from a nervous condition caused by his fear of his teacher. They said that the day before, Mrs. Donald hit Dick and he fell into a desk and bruised his arm.

Background:

Mrs. Donald has the reputation of being an excellent teacher with the exception of her interpersonal relations with some children. She has been known to call children "stupid," to lose her temper, and to hit children. Several parents have requested that their children not be placed in her class, or that they be removed from her class. The previous administrators had defended her behavior to the parents, although they had at times removed the child at the parent's request. Mrs. Donald has never been written up for any incident.

Questions:

1. How would you deal with Dick's parents?
2. Would you remove Dick from Mrs. Donald's class?
3. As the principal, you know what Mrs. Donald has done. How would you respond?
4. How can any administrator defend abusive teacher behavior?
5. As a new principal to this school, you have no history with Mrs. Donald. How do you get the information you need to take action?
6. Can you respond to situations like this even when no documentation exists?
7. What are the legal ramifications of this incident?

References:

Cook, J. 1996. Helping abused students. *Teaching PreK-8* 26:60-61.
Dayton, J. 1994. Corporal punishment in public schools: The legal and political battle continues. *West's Education Law Quarterly* 3:448-459.

Robinson, E.H. et al. 1990. Coping with fears and stress. An activity guide: Grades K-8. ED328832.
Schulz, C.D. 1996. What really frightens children in school? *Educational Horizons* 74:139-144.

63. STUDENT INSUBORDINATION

Problem:

A teacher has hall duty at the end of class. Two junior-high students are outside of the room they are supposed to be in. The teacher asks both students to return to the class. The students do not move. The teacher says, "Are you deaf? Get back in the room." One student goes back, the other one just stands there. The teacher then says, "Are you going to stand there like a schmuck or are you going to move?" The student replies defiantly, "I guess I'm going to be a schmuck." The teacher then writes up the student for insubordination.

Background:

The teacher is highly thought of and has had no problems in the past. This is also the teacher's tenure year. The student has a partial hearing loss in his right ear (not known to the teacher) and is said to have taken offense to the teacher asking, "Are you deaf?". The student has no past discipline problems.

Questions:

1. How would you handle the teacher?
2. What sort of punishment, if any, should the insubordinate student receive?
3. Should this incident have any effect on the teacher's tenure?
4. What should you say to the student's parents?

References:

Crone, L.J., and C. Teddlie. 1995. Further examination of teacher behavior in differentially effective schools: Selection and socialization process. *Journal of Classroom Instruction* 30:1-9.
Educational Testing Service. 1990. Classroom interaction. Annotated bibliography of tests. ED369825.

Freeman, J.G. 1994. An adolescent with learning disabilities, Eric: The perspective of a potential dropout. *Canadian Journal of Special Education* 9:131-147.

Lawrence, C.E., and M.K. Vachon. 1995. How to handle staff misconduct: A step-by-step guide. ED377569.

64. STUDENT PHYSICALLY THREATENING TEACHER

Problem:

You, the principal, were called to the classroom of Mrs. Ramirez, the ESL teacher. When you entered the room you found Jose holding a chair in a very threatening manner. You were able to convince the student to put the chair down and to accompany you to the office. During the follow-up investigation you learned that Jose had been disruptive in class and had threatened the teacher to the point of picking up the chair. This was not the first incident of disruptive behavior on the part of this student.

Background:

Jose recently arrived from Puerto Rico. When he went to school in Puerto Rico he did not attend beyond the fourth grade. At present he is in the eighth grade and does not speak any English. He has no desire to learn English because when you are a member of a gang it is not necessary to learn to speak English. One brother is in jail for murder in Puerto Rico and the other is in jail locally for blowing up a police car.

Questions:

1. What will be the immediate punishment for Jose's behavior?
2. What actions will you take with Jose in the future (e.g., alternative program, psychological testing, etc.)?
3. Who else will you involve in developing an improvement plan?
4. How will you deal with Jose's parents?
5. What steps will you take to uncover any gang activities going on in your school?

References:

Ayres, B.J., and D.L. Hedeen. 1996. Been there, done that, didn't work: Alternative solutions for behavior problems. *Educational Leadership* 53:48-50.

Baron, E.B. 1992. Discipline strategies for teachers. Fastback 344. ED356201.

Gillum, L.R., Jr. 1995. Reducing verbal and physically abusive behaviors of ninth through twelfth grade students through a structured support group process. ED383969.

Henderson, J., and B. Friedland. 1996. Suspension, a wake-up call. Rural educators' attitudes toward suspension. ED394749.

Keeping our schools safe: A survey of teachers and students about violence in U.S. Schools. 1994. ED374118.

65. STUDENT SELLING STOLEN CANDY

Problem:

A cafeteria supervisor observed a seventh-grade female student with a shopping bag full of "store bought" candy. The student was openly selling the candy to her classmates. When questioned by the teacher, the student's story was that she bought it.

Background:

A search of her locker by her teacher (admittedly illegal) uncovered two similar shopping bags. The total estimated value of the three bags of candy exceeded forty dollars. When interrogated by the dean, the student admitted shoplifting the candy (along with three eleven-year-old friends) from a local supermarket. The candy mob bicycled from their homes to the store and simply "loaded up and walked out" each time.

Questions:

1. What action(s) will you take with the students involved?
2. How will you deal with their parents?
3. What will you do about the teacher's illegal locker search?
4. What will you do about the store where the candy was stolen?
5. Whom do you need to consult regarding this issue?

References:

Lincoln, E.A. 1995. Searches and seizures in public schools. ED392157.

McKinney, J.R. 1994. The fourth amendment and the public schools: Reasonable suspicion in the 1990s. *West's Education Law Quarterly* 3:591-599.

Sendor, B. 1996. A swift and sure student search. *American School Board Journal* 183:11, 39.

Valenza, J. 1995. Steps to simplifying student searches. *Technology Connection* 2:21-22.

66. STUDENT/STUDENT SEXUAL ASSAULT

Problem:

At 9:00 a.m., a very angry Mrs. Black stormed into your office shouting that her son Anthony had told her that yesterday morning he had witnessed Francisco Rico exposing himself on the bus and forcing a younger child to perform oral sex on him. She insisted on knowing if Francisco was going to be allowed to continue to ride the bus. You, the principal, had just been informed of the exposure incident by the director of special education at 8:40 that morning. No mention had been made of an act of oral sex. You have not received a written report from the bus staff on this incident. Bus reports are due in your office within 24 hours.

Background:

Anthony is an eleven-year-old student with neurological and emotional handicaps. He is an extroverted, acting-out child who has a history of sexual overtness. Francisco Rico is a thirteen-year-old student with emotional handicaps. The professional staff who work closely with Francisco have indicated great concern for his apparent emotional and psychological deterioration. They have expressed great concern about his provocative language and sexual advances toward his new young female teacher.

Questions:

1. How would you deal with Mrs. Black?
2. What action would you take with Francisco?
3. How would you deal with his mother?

4. What would you do relative to the bus situation and the lateness of the report?

References:

Bachus, G.S., and D.H. Wright. 1996. Student-to-student sexual harassment: How serious is the problem? *ERS Spectrum* 14:3-6.

Cohen, A. et al. 1996. Sexual harassment and sexual abuse: A handbook for teachers and administrators. ED396429.

Deel, T. et al. 1991. Student sexual abuse: An administrative nightmare. ED331170.

Drugge, J.E. 1992. Perceptions of child sexual assault. *Journal of Offender Rehabilitation* 18:141-165.

Simon, T.B., and C.A. Harris. 1993. Sex without consent. Ed378505.

67. STUDENTS LEAVING SCHOOL WITHOUT PERMISSION

Problem:

Yesterday the assistant principal prevented two middle-school students, John Scales and Billy Jones, from getting on the school bus at the end of the day. The students were told that since they left school earlier, they were not entitled to school transportation home. At that time both students were told of their assigned in-school detention the next day.

Background:

Three teachers and several students saw John and Billy leaving the school building at approximately 1:00 p.m. They were reported to be running in the direction of the store complex across the street from the school. The assistant principal successfully contacted Mrs. Scales and informed her that John had left school illegally and that he would be assigned in-school detention the next day. The assistant principal was unable to contact Mrs. Jones. School was dismissed at 2:40 p.m. and the two boys returned to school from the shopping complex and attempted to board the school bus.

This morning Mrs. Jones calls you, the principal, for an appointment and informs you that Billy did not cut school, but was picked up by her and then dropped off by her at the end of the school day in order to take the bus home. You inform her of the witnesses that saw him leave school and the testimony of the other student involved in the incident. Mrs. Jones insists that she picked him up.

Questions:

1. How will you deal with Billy?
2. How will you deal with Mrs. Jones?
3. How will you make sure that both boys receive equally fair treatment?
4. What rules will you establish for the rest of the students to prevent this incident from being repeated?

References:

Bobbitt, S.A., and C.L. Rohr. 1993. What are the most serious problems in schools? Issue Brief. ED355620.

Cicchelli, T. et al. 1990. Dropout prevention strategies for urban children at-risk: A longitudinal analysis. ED347213.

Harte, A.J. 1995. Improving school attendance. ED383042.

Hernan, J.L. 1991. Developing a procedure for accountability of student absenteeism. ED340144.

Student absenteeism and tardiness. Indicator of the month. 1996. ED396461.

68. TEACHER ALCOHOLISM AND SEXUAL BEHAVIOR

Problem:

During the past year, many parents have been voicing concern about the wisdom of having an alcoholic teacher in the classroom. On several occasions, parents have complained that, according to their children, Miss Jones is coming to school with alcohol on her breath. Some parents have voiced concern about her sexual attire and mannerisms in the classroom. For example, students were bringing home stories about how the teacher sits on her desk with crossed legs and teaches from that position. In addition, the parents of some eighth-grade boys claim she is making improper advances toward their sons.

Background:

Miss Jones is a tenured English teacher with fifteen years of service in the school district. During this time, she has performed very well. Miss Jones is a sociable person and has many friends on the staff. She is also the shop steward for the teachers' union.

The principal and many of the teachers are aware that Miss Jones has a drinking problem. She has been informally counseled several times concerning her coming to school with alcohol on her breath. At the time, this was not considered a serious problem, since it did not affect her teaching.

Questions:

1. What plan of action will you develop with Miss Jones regarding her behavior?
2. Considering the denial commonly exhibited by alcoholics, what external sources will you turn to for assistance?
3. How will you involve other administrators in the district?
4. How will you respond to the parents' concerns?

References:

An employer's guide to dealing with substance abuse. 1990. ED332095.

Esplund, D.L. 1994. Factors associated with attitude toward alcohol in small high schools. ED376391.

Harris, R.C., and C.M. Hawkins. 1989. Substance abuse in the workplace: Implications for trade and industry education. ED318880.

Smith, D.A. 1993. A cross-disciplinary integrative summary of research on workplace substance abuse. ED366870.

Watts, W.D., and A.P. Short. 1990. Teacher drug use: A response to occupational stress. *Journal of Drug Education* 20:47-65.

69. TEACHER DISMISSAL

Problem:

Three junior-high school faculty members have asked you, the principal, to stop what they consider to be highly disruptive and unprofessional behavior on the part of Mr. Malone, the K-8 physical-education teacher. The three teachers have allotted their lunch breaks as time during which remedial assistance is provided for students who have been falling behind in their studies. For approximately one month, Mr. Malone has been making daily observations of the three teachers during their lunchtime. Each day at the same time, he walks past each of their three classrooms and stops in the doorway to watch whatever is going on. It is quite obvious that he takes notes during each visit. After unsuccessful attempts to end Mr. Malone's actions, through personally confronting him and requesting that he stop, the three teachers have referred their problem to you.

Background:

Mr. Malone is presently the subject of a disciplinary action. You have initiated two hearings in an effort to have him dismissed. In the first hearing, he was found guilty of punching an eighth-grade boy in the face during a physical-education class and was suspended for one month without pay. After the second hearing, Mr. Malone was suspended for one half year without pay because he had unjustly failed more than 50 percent of his students for noncompliance with the dress code. He had not made any attempts to offer remedial help to them as per district policy.

Mr. Malone's daily observing is a way of collecting information for his defense in his latest hearing. You had stated at one hearing that teachers who have a high percentage of students with failing grades have offered remedial help to these students during their lunchtime. When confronted by one teacher, Mr. Malone insisted he would continue to collect information for his defense in any way he saw fit. He also stated that he was engaged in other types of surveillance of which the teachers and administrators were unaware.

Questions:

1. What action should you take with Mr. Malone regarding his observing the three teachers at lunchtime?
2. Write a memo to Mr. Malone describing the problem and directing him to take specific action to stop his observations.
3. What are the other issues involved in this case study? What action should you take to solve those issues?
4. How will you handle the concerns of the other three teachers who are under surveillance?
5. Whom will you consult regarding Mr. Malone's current behavior?

References:

Andrews, H.A. 1992. How to dismiss a tenured faculty member. *Administrative Action* 4:1-5.

Grant, C.M. 1995. Predismissal hearings for school employees: Developments since "Loudermill." *School Law Bulletin* 26:1-9.

Menacker, J. 1995. A dilemma in teacher dismissal hearings: Determining what is right when both sides are wrong. *West's Education Law Quarterly* 4:63-73.

Pratt, F. 1996. The ethical principal and teacher nonretention. Journal of *Personnel Evaluation in Education* 10:29-36.

VanSciver, J.H. 1990. Teacher dismissals. *Phi Delta Kappan* 72:318-319.

70. TEACHER FAILURE TO REPORT TO SUMMER-SCHOOL ASSIGNMENT

Problem:

Ms. Thomas has been hired to teach a special-education class for a six-week summer-school session. Classes are to begin on Monday, July 10 at 8:00 a.m. At 6:45 a.m. on July 10, Ms. Thomas calls to inform you that she is not going to be able to start today because of personal problems. Later the same day she calls your secretary and tells her she will not be in until Wednesday morning, July 12.

Background:

Ms. Thomas has come to you with high recommendations from one of your neighboring districts. She has been a teacher for ten years and has no past record of this type. When asked over the phone what the problem is you are told she will not talk about it over the phone.

Questions:

1. How will you deal with Ms. Thomas?
2. What recourse do you have?
3. How will you cover the class today when there are no substitutes available?
4. What will you do about the class for the rest of the summer-school session?

References:

Brownell, M.T., and S.W. Smith. 1993. Understanding special education teacher attrition: A conceptual model and implications for teacher educators. *Teacher Education and Special Education* 16:270-282.

Cohen, M.K. et al. 1994. Survival guide for the first-year special education teacher. Revised edition. ED375569.

Matlock, J. 1992. Solving the problem of problem employees. *Executive Educator* 14:39-40.

McCabe, M. 1995. How principals can help the beginning special education teacher. *NASSP Bulletin* 79:1-14.

Wright, J. 1995. Transforming summer school: Creating a quality classroom. *Teaching and Change* 2:218-229.

71. TEACHER REASSSIGNMENT

Problem:

The lack of student participation in band at the middle-school level has made a great impact on the high-school band program. In order to remedy this situation, Mr. Nolan was pulled out of the instrumental program this summer and assigned to five periods of general music. Mr. Nolan has never taught in a classroom setting. Due to his poor classroom management, he has had several confrontations with students leading to student suspensions. There is a particular period in which the assistant principal has to sit in his classroom every day to keep order. Mr. Nolan constantly calls the office to complain about the students in his classes.

Background:

Mr. Nolan has been the band director at this middle school for the last twenty years. He has worked in the district for twenty-eight years. For the last ten years he has served as a union building representative or alternate. Mr. Nolan's ability to handle the band students has been deteriorating in the past four to five years. Each year the number of students joining the band has decreased. The students complain about his temper. He has been known to yell excessively at students and insult them by using terms such as "scumbag," "low-life," and "dirtbag." He has reportedly thrown furniture around. There have been a number of student and parental complaints against him at the building level as well as at central office. He has been called in for conferences with the assistant principal, the former principal, the assistant superintendent for instruction, and the superintendent. This is your first year as the middle-school principal.

Questions:

1. What course of action should you take in dealing with this situation?
2. What can you do to improve Mr. Nolan's behavior and build up the middle-school band program?
3. Develop an improvement plan for Mr. Nolan.
4. What actions will you take regarding parent and student complaints?

References:

Johnstone, M. 1993. Teachers' workload and associated stress. ED368716.

Nweze, B.R. 1993. Increasing parent involvement, student attendance and appropriate school behavior of at-risk middle school students through parent partnerships. ED366485.

Reyes, R., and M. Imber. 1992. Teachers' perceptions of the fairness of their workload and their commitment, job satisfaction, and morale: Implications for teacher evaluation. *Journal of Personnel Evaluation in Education* 5:291-302.

Vockell, E. L. 1996. When parents complain about bad teachers. *School Community Journal* 6:127-129.

72. TEACHER SENIORITY DURING DECLINING ENROLLMENT

Problem:

You are the principal of Wells Junior High School in a large central school district (there are two senior high schools and three junior high schools). Due to declining enrollment, you are going to lose an English teaching position, but no one will lose a job since it will be offset by attrition. However, someone will have to be transferred to another building. Having assessed the relative merits of all potential transfers, you believe that Mr. Adams, the least senior teacher in your English department, is a more integral part of your program and contributes significantly more, both quantitatively and qualitatively, than the next least senior teacher. Mr. Adams is young, cooperative, conscientious, and serves as student-government advisor. The next least senior teacher, Mrs. Miller, is twenty years older, is often late to school and to classes, uncooperative, has a difficult personality, is frequently absent, has difficulty with less capable students and minorities, and wants no part of any extracurricular assignments. Your staff has presented you with a petition urging you to follow the contract and observe the least senior teacher clause.

Background:

As building principal you have the primary responsibility for programs and quality of instruction. However, a major constraint of this situation includes the contract with the teachers that states, with regard to involuntary transfer, "All other factors being equal, teachers with greatest seniority in the school district shall be last to be transferred involuntarily."

Precedents in the district include a number of reassignments resulting from declining enrollments. In some instances grievances were filed by the affected teacher(s) and in at least three cases went to arbitration. In each of the cases that went to arbitration, where the district had relied on "all other factors being equal" and transferred someone other than the least senior teacher, the decision was upheld in favor of the district.

Questions:

1. What would your decision be regarding which teacher is to be moved and why?
2. If you decide to transfer the second least senior teacher, how could you explain your decision to the teachers' association representatives so that they will support you?
3. What impact and restrictions do teacher contracts sometimes have on a principal when he/she is making personnel decisions?

References:

Boe, E.E. 1990. Comprehensive retention and attrition model (CRAM). ED328527.

Goodell, A.L. 1992. Striking is hard to do: The structuration of school climate during teacher contract negotiations. ED357394.

Murphy, J. 1993. What's in? What's out? American education in the nineties. *Phi Delta Kappan* 74:641-646.

Peace, N.E. 1994. A new way to negotiate-collaborative bargaining in teacher contract negotiations: The experience in five Massachusetts school districts. *Journal of Law and Education* 23:365-379.

73. TEACHER STALKED

Problem:

Ms. Ramey has been employed as a teacher in your junior-high summer school for four weeks. This morning, you witnessed a bitter argument in the parking lot before the beginning of school between Ms. Ramey and an unidentified male. You met Ms. Ramey entering the building; she was crying and asked to speak to you at once. Ms. Ramey explained that the male is her former boyfriend and he is stalking her. She says that he has followed her here to school and she is not sure what he is planning to do.

Background:

Ms. Ramey outlined to you that she is going through a breakup and it is a nasty one. Your building is open and not secured because of the summer heat.

Questions:

1. How should you proceed?
2. What measures can you put in place to protect the safety of the students?
3. Who else should you consult?
4. How can you support Mrs. Ramey without getting in the middle of her problem?

References:

Hoffman, A.M., ed. 1996. Schools, violence, and society. ED399618.
Modzeleski, W. 1996. Creating safe schools: Roles and challenges, a federal perspective. *Education and Urban Society* 28:412-423.
Rossi, R., and S. Daugherty. 1996. How safe are the public schools: What do teachers say? Issue Brief. ED396430.
Safe schools: A handbook for practitioners. 1996. ED399619.

74. TEACHER WITH EMOTIONAL PROBLEMS

Problem:

Mr. Peters is a junior-high teacher. It has become increasingly obvious that he has emotional problems. These problems are affecting his relationships with his colleagues and students. He refuses to communicate with his students for days on end if he feels that they have not behaved properly. Then there are other days he is unusually warm and helpful. It has been noted that there is a marked decline in the enrollment of his elective course. Mr. Andrews, his department chairman, is concerned about this drop in class enrollment since the course of study is not state mandated and he doesn't want the board of education to find reasons to cut the program. Also, Mr. Andrews is concerned with the effects of Mr. Peter's erratic behavior on the students.

Background:

Mr. Peters has tenure but the emotional problem was evident while he was still untenured. The department chairman and the former principal did not document the problem because they felt it might hurt Mr. Peter's future in education.

Questions:

1. What are the basic problem(s) in this case study?
2. How can you, the principal, help this teacher?
3. How can the department chairman help save this course?
4. What assistance would you provide this teacher? Who would you use as resources?

References:

O'Neil, I., and D.R. Adamson. 1993. When teachers falter. *Executive Educator* 15:25-27.

Poole, W. 1995. Reconstructing the teacher-administrator relationship to achieve systematic change. *Journal of School Leadership* 5:565-596.

Swain, B. 1994. Your workplace: An emotional battlefield? *Child Care Information Exchange* 96:73-76.

75. TEACHER WITH WORK-RELATED INJURIES

Problem:

Mrs. Xavier was hired after the school term had begun, when an additional position needed to be filled. Her program consists of one junior-high English, one reading, and three math classes.

Unfortunately, Mrs. Xavier is now chronically absent due to "work-related injuries." Shortly after she began teaching, she claimed to have slipped on a jelly donut in class. She filed an accident report and was absent for several days without calling to notify the school that she would be out. When she returned, Mrs. Xavier was late several times, missing part of her first class. After about a week, she was absent again, did not call the school, and had someone notify an assistant principal that she had suffered a miscarriage. She returned to school for a few days and then was absent again, claiming the death of her father. When school personnel called her house, they received confusing messages by relatives as to Mrs. Xavier's absence. A few days after Mrs. Xavier returned, she was hit on the side of the neck by a student in one of her classes. She was absent the next day to appear in court. Following that day, she has not returned to school.

Background:

Mrs. Xavier is in her late twenties. When marks were due, she sent someone to the school to pick up her report cards. During her conference with the English department chairman, she has been very agreeable and open to suggestions about her work. However, during conferences about her attendance with you, the principal, she has been hostile and adamant about her right to take days off.

Questions:

1. List the major problems concerning Mrs. Xavier.
2. Describe what you would do to solve these problems.
3. If Mrs. Xavier does not return to school, what action will you take?
4. What other sources will you consult?

References:

Boyer, C.E. 1994. The relationship between buy-back provisions and teacher attendance rates. ED384972.

Kleine, P.A. 1994. Chronic absenteeism: A community issue. ED375494.

Unicomb, R. et al. 1992. Teacher absenteeism. A study of short-term teacher absenteeism in nine Nova Scotia schools, which shows that teachers are absent significantly less than workers in others professions. *Education Canada* 32:33-37.

White, N.A. 1990. Cut sick-pay a day: An incentive plan to reduce teacher absenteeism. A practicum report. ED324806.

76. TEACHERS' INABILITY TO SHARE CLASSROOM

Problem:

Mrs. Brown, a Spanish teacher who shares the same classroom with Mrs. Davis, has been coming to you with concerns about broken and missing items in the classroom (pencil sharpener, stapler, scissors, etc.). Mrs. Brown also notices how messy the room is when Mrs. Davis has finished teaching her class in there (mud, paper on the floor, gum, writing on the desks and spit balls all around the room). Mrs. Brown has now taken down all of her bulletin boards because they were slowly being destroyed. Mrs. Brown says she has spoken to Mrs. Davis, but things never change.

Recently, a concerned citizen has come to you with complaints that while he was jogging by the school, students in Mrs. Davis' classroom yelled obscenities at him. Parents have been calling and other teachers are complaining that the students who passed her class last year are entering their Spanish classes this year totally unprepared and frustrated.

Background:

Mrs. Davis has been a Spanish teacher in the district for over twenty years. She has taught mostly at the high-school level, but recently she has had a few classes at the junior high school. During her years of teaching, she has had serious trouble with classroom management. She has been spoken to about this problem and has been offered help by administrators. However, she has refused all assistance. Parents have been concerned with the lack of control in her classroom and the students' unpreparedness for the next level of Spanish after completing her class.

Questions:

1. As principal, how do you react to parents when they call with concerns about a teacher's lack of control and poor instruction?
2. How do you address Mrs. Davis with these issues?
3. What would you do if Mrs. Davis refuses help?
4. How can you provide support to Mrs. Brown?

5. What do you say to the teachers who are complaining about the students' lack of preparation?

References:

Baird, J.R. 1994. Classroom collaboration to diagnose and improve the quality of teaching and learning. ED375120.

Leadership for collaboration: Participant's workbook. 1993. ED366457.

McCammon, L.A. 1994. Teamwork is not just a word: Factors disrupting the development of a departmental group of theatre teachers. *Youth Theatre Journal* 8:3-9.

Rodgers, C.R. et al. 1993. Mentoring each other: Teacher educators as learners of teaching. ED362509.

77. TEACHING STYLE

Problem:

Mr. and Mrs. Swanson have requested that their daughter be moved out of Mr. Johnson's social-studies class and put into another teacher's class. Their complaint is that Mr. Johnson's class consists of nothing but memorizing pages of isolated facts that he copies and passes out. He does not use a text and they say that there is no evidence of history being taught. The Swansons' daughter complains bitterly about the course and "all the memorization." Her parents have already discussed their concern with the teacher as you requested. There has been no change. They are back again with their request, insisting that their daughter be changed to another teacher who teaches history and incorporates critical thinking and writing assignments into the course. A review of the girl's record shows that she is an excellent student; her average grade is above 90. The change can be made with no disruption to her schedule, as there is room in the other class. Mr. and Mrs. Swanson have told you that they "are hoping not to have to take their request to the school board."

Background:

Mr. Johnson is a seventh-grade social-studies teacher. He is very pleasant; parents rarely, if ever, voice a complaint against him. Students tend to do well in his class. His class, however, has consisted of pure memorization of facts for the three years that you have been in the building.

Questions:

1. As building principal will you change the girl's teacher?
2. What will you say to the Swansons?
3. What will you say to Mr. Johnson?
4. What are the long-range problems associated with moving students out of a teacher's class?

References:

Issacs, E. 1995. Learning to value our different styles. ED395326.
Teaching style. Annotated bibliography of tests. 1990. ED369804.

78. TEAM TEACHING

Problem:

Mr. Landers is a teacher in a self-contained middle-school special-education classroom. He enjoys teaching science and has a menagerie of tropical fish, reptiles, and pet rodents in his room. After over twenty years of teaching, Mr. Landers is reluctant to participate in an inclusionary team-teaching program.

Background:

Mr. Landers gives packets of work to students every day that take about one-and-a-half hours to complete. After this is done, students may play with the animals, watch movies, and have "free time." Mr. Landers believes that he provides an individualized program and has difficulty understanding and accepting suggestions from you, the principal, about group lessons, thematic units, and interdisciplinary teaching.

Questions:

1. What directives do you need to give Mr. Landers?
2. How will you know if he has implemented your suggestions and directives?
3. What strategies will you use to integrate his class into a team-teaching program?

References:

Clapsaddle, J., and J. Thomas. 1991. A healthy start for team teaching. *Vocational Education Journal* 66:28-29.

Morganti, D.J., and F.C. Buckalew. 1991. The benefits of team teaching. *Research Strategies* 9:195-197.

Russell, S.C. et al. 1994. Teachers teaching teachers: The art of working together and sharing. ED369616.

Thomas, G. 1991. Defining role in the new classroom teams. *Educational Research* 33:186-198.

79. UNFAIR STUDENT PUNISHMENT

Problem:

The day after the sixth-grade parent-teacher conferences, Kevin Lawson's parents call and ask to meet with you. Kevin's social-studies teacher, Mr. James, informed them at their conference the previous night that Kevin and some other students had left the class by the time he arrived to teach on a given day. Mr. James told the parents he had arrived five minutes late to class after receiving an emergency phone call. When the parents questioned Kevin immediately following the conference, Kevin complained that Mr. James was actually fifteen to twenty minutes late for the forty-minute class on the given day, and the student believed he would not arrive at all. His parents suggested that he should have gone to an administrator or to them to report this. Kevin responded that the students had not done so because they feared repercussions from Mr. James if they "reported him," since Mr. James has demonstrated a short temper in the past. Kevin explained in his discussion with his parents and also with you, the principal, that Mr. James has been late many times (five or more) throughout the semester and always has an excuse for his class (phone calls, car trouble, etc.). Other students in the class have verified such statements.

Background:

Mr. James is a tenured teacher who has taught in the building for five years. The administrators and teachers stress the importance of punctuality and attendance and students face consequences for tardiness and illegal absences. Since this incident, reports have been made by other students in this and other classes of Mr. James arriving late, failing to keep accurate grade books (he was unable to justify students' grades), unprofessional attire, lack of cleanliness, and limited temper control.

Questions:

1. How do you relieve parental concerns about lack of supervision of the child and loss of educational time?
2. What do you do to make students feel you are accessible to them and an advocate for them? How do you encourage them to report incidents in a timely manner so they can be dealt with effectively?
3. How do you address Mr. James concerning the above issues? What specific actions will you take regarding his inappropriate and unprofessional behavior?
4. What actions will you take with the students who left the class?

References:

Alley, R. et al. 1990. Student misbehaviors: Which ones really trouble teachers? *Teacher Education Quarterly* 17:63-70.

French, D. et al. 1991. A focus on discipline and attendance. Structuring schools for student success. ED336843.

Gordon, W.M. 1995. The search for reasonableness: Legal issues in student discipline. *School Business Affairs* 61:18-21.

Murphy, C. 1995. Managing students: Building positive attitudes in the classroom. *Schools in the Middle* 4:31-33.

Pressman, R., and S. Weinstein. 1990. Procedural due process rights in student discipline. ED334652.

CHAPTER FIVE

High-School Case Studies

At the high-school level, any personnel problem quickly becomes public knowledge and very often finds its way into the local press, causing numerous problems for the high-school principal and central office administration. High-school students often know about teacher incidents before the administrators, which can cause embarrassment, legal problems, and negative public relations. It is at this level that teachers sometimes become inappropriately involved with students, violating the standard teacher-student relationship. At a time when students are trying to define who they are and what they want to do with their lives, it is essential that teachers serve as role models and not as the source of anxiety. Teachers should not add to the problems that many students of this age are dealing with in their home and school lives. The high-school principal must be vigilant in knowing what is happening with the personnel in the school and deal with problems involving teachers, students, parents, and support staff immediately and judiciously in order to preserve the integrity of the school and its mission.

This chapter on high-school case studies includes teacher problems that address absenteeism; name-calling; assaulting a student; classroom observation problems; refusal to serve as advisor; withholding a grade for a graduating senior; incompetence; lack of security at the junior prom; teacher imposition of pro-choice attitudes; teacher reaction to budget defeat; dealing with teacher union complaints about supervisory practices; abusive behavior; a teacher-student affair; teacher burn-out; erratic behavior; practicing law during school time; attrition rates in foreign-language classes; racism; a request for preferential scheduling;

homosexuality; termination of a probationary teacher; and low passing scores on statewide exams.

Parent problems are reflected in case studies that include demands of a parent "Committee for Academic Excellence;" complaints about new courses; use of personal influence; and accusation of a teacher hitting a student.

Cases that address student problems include absence for abortion; uncooperative student behavior during an emergency; suspension of special-education students; inappropriate cheerleader behavior; graffiti at a rival school during a sports event; a stolen final exam; athletes drinking; breaking up a student fight; teenage pregnancy; and yearbook policies including student freedom of expression.

80. ATTRITION RATE IN FOREIGN-LANGUAGE CLASSES

Problem:

Mrs. Bryce is a secondary Spanish teacher who has taught in the district for approximately fifteen years. She is extremely knowledgeable and well organized, but her high standards discourage a significant number of students. As a consequence, the attrition rate in her classes is much higher than in other classes at the same level. Those students who persevere, however, tend to do well on the standardized final examination. When questioned about the large number of her students who received failing grades and/or dropped Spanish early in the year, Mrs. Bryce placed the blame on the teacher who had them the year before. The students, she said, were just not adequately prepared. This year Mrs. Bryce has been assigned to a beginning-level Spanish course.

Mrs. Bryce's dominant personality and lack of flexibility also influence her relationships with other department members. With few exceptions, her self-confidence and her sharp tongue intimidate the other teachers. Her negative attitude toward change has adversely affected recent meetings on revision of the final examinations and on the adoption of a new textbook.

Background:

When Mrs. Bryce began teaching, foreign-language classes were filled with college-bound students who were highly motivated to do well. There were so many of them, in fact, that there was not room for less able learners. Over the past years, many colleges have eliminated foreign-language entrance examinations, and most secondary schools have suffered a decline in enrollment.

Questions:

1. Describe Mrs. Bryce's problems.
2. How would you, as principal, address each of these problems?
3. What resources are available to help assist Mrs. Bryce in her improvement plan?
4. What implications does this situation have for the foreign-language program?

References:

Campbell, K.P. 1991. Personal norms of experienced expert suburban high school teachers: Implications for selecting and retaining outstanding individuals. *Action in Teacher Education* 12:35-40.

Henderson, J.C. 1990. The relationship between teachers' personality factors and their compliance with administrative directives. ED331163.

Sparks, R., and R.P. Lipka. 1992. Characteristics of master teachers: Personality factors, self-concept, locus of control, and pupil control ideology. *Journal of Personnel Evaluation in Education* 5:303-311.

Wood, P.H. et al. 1990. Grading and evaluation practices and policies of school teachers. ED319782.

81. BREAKING UP A STUDENT FIGHT

Problem:

A student has just punched you, the principal of Castleton High School, in the head as you intervened to break up a fight. Your assistant principal is on his way to the hospital in an ambulance because he has just been thrown over a car in the parking lot while also attempting to bring the fight to a halt. He has a heart condition and is being taken in for observation. The police are on the scene and three students have been taken into custody.

Background:

Three students from the high school cut classes and went drinking. They came back at dismissal time with the intention of fighting three other students with whom they had been feuding for several months. The first three students taunted those who had remained in school until a fight broke out. There have been numerous fights in the school in the last two months and most have been initiated by these two groups. A further problem exists because other students run to watch. Some students take sides and also begin fighting, thus escalating the violence.

Questions:

1. What discipline procedures will you follow with the three students who initiated the fight?
2. How will you handle other students who participated?
3. What procedures will you follow in order to bring these confrontations to an end?
4. Whom will you consult regarding the prevention of future confrontations?

References:

Bullock, L.M., and R.A. Gable, eds. 1995. Perspectives on school aggression and violence. ED391338.

Curcio, J.L., and P.F. First. 1993. Violence in the schools: How to proactively prevent and defuse it. Roadmaps to success: The practicing administrator's leadership series. ED358548.

Duhon-Sells, R., ed. 1995. Dealing with youth violence. What schools and communities need to know. ED395096.

Petersen, G.J. et al. 1996. The enemy from within: A national study on school violence and prevention. ED394907.

Safe schools survey. Post-secondary student survey. 1996. ED396660.

82. CLASSROOM OBSERVATION OF SPECIAL-EDUCATION TEACHER

Problem:

Mr. Holmes was observed by the assistant principal in his special-education class. It took the class approximately 30 minutes to complete what should have been a five-to ten-minute exercise. The lesson had to do with the vocabulary of shopping and making change. Mr. Holmes relied totally on the book. One student attempted to sabotage the lesson by asking irrelevant questions. The goals of the lesson were not met.

Background:

Mr. Holmes has been a special-education teacher in an inner-city high school for ten years. He has never received an unsatisfactory rating. His daily appearance is disheveled and unkempt. There is no dress code in the city school. Although he spends hours preparing his lessons, his papers are always flying all over the place; rarely are two papers facing the same way in his daily book. Mr. Holmes' classroom management techniques are equal to his organizational skills. Frequently, fights break out in his class. The only time his classes are calm is when the paraprofessional is present. You feel that the only reason students have not complained about Mr. Holmes is because it is almost impossible to receive a failing grade from him.

Questions:

1. What are the critical problems in this case? List the problems from the most critical to least critical.
2. Select two areas of concern and develop an improvement plan for each of them.
3. Write a scenario for conferring with Mr. Holmes.

References:

Block, D.M. 1993. Authentic video and classroom observation. *System* 21:49-67.

Hopkins, W. S., and K.D. Moore. 1995. Clinical supervision: A neo-progressive approach. *Teacher Educator* 30:31-43.

Huntington, F. 1995. Management by mingling revisited. *Executive Educator* 17:30-31.

Kim, M.Y., and G. Sugai. 1995. The effects of self-evaluation, self-observation, and self-observation plus self-recording on the occurrence of disruptive behaviors in classroom: Extension study. ED385028.

Weade, G., and C.M. Evertson. 1991. On what can be learned by observing teaching: *Theory into Practice* 30:37-45.

83. DEFEAT OF SPORTS/EXTRACURRICULAR PORTION OF SCHOOL BUDGET

Problem:

The school year at Vernon High School began without sports or extracurricular activities as that part of the school budget had been defeated. Thus, no athletic events, dances, or club activities will be held at Vernon this year. The faculty association feels it cannot support the Booster Club activities and that teachers, in light of the budget defeat, should not volunteer to head organizations for which compensation was paid in the past. You, as the principal of Vernon, however, have made it clear that despite the stand taken by the teachers' association, you have an obligation to organize and support as many school activities as possible. You also feel it is your responsibility to encourage faculty members to volunteer their time and services to school activities.

Background:

The defeat of the sports and extracurricular portion of the Vernon budget came after four budget votes. The latest defeat by only six votes occurred the first week of September. A community money drive was organized. The faculty association's failure to support the drive, as well as its unwillingness to coach and advise on a volunteer basis, were unpopular stands with many students, parents, and community members. All in all, it is a time of tension at Vernon.

Questions:

1. What other strategies could you develop to reinstate at least some of the school activities lost through four budget defeats?
2. How would you deal with the faculty association?
3. What are the long-term public relations implications for this situation and what actions could you take in this matter?

References:

Bolick, N.O. 1991. School budget blues. *American School Board Journal* 178:34-36.

Campbell, G. 1995. Drawing the community into the school district budget. *School Business Affairs* 61:9-13.

Disario, P. 1987. The board and the budget: What every school board member should know about sound school financial management. ED324824.

Greaser, T.C., Jr. 1994. Alternative teaching strategies to improve instrumental lesson instruction at the middle school, when the budget has been reduced. ED377115.

Shortt, T.L. 1994. Teachers can become a vital component of the school budget process. *NASSP Bulletin* 78:39-46.

84. DEMANDS OF PARENT "COMMITTEE FOR ACADEMIC EXCELLENCE"

Problem:

As high-school principal in a very diverse school district, you receive a letter from a "group of concerned parents" calling themselves the "Committee for Academic Excellence." They are not associated with any existing PTA or other recognized school parents' group. They express their concern over the "lack of challenge to academically gifted children" and the "lack of contest winners, such as the Westinghouse science competition," by the district. They demand a list of items including: SAT scores for all students taking the exam; IQ's of district students; description of ongoing district committees and their constituency; organizational chart; academic programs studied or adopted; names and phone numbers of all district administrators; and a description of each school's support services, their function, and target population.

Background:

This committee had meetings and passed out literature asking for more involvement from other concerned parents. You are very suspicious of a hidden agenda and the membership of this group. You also question their motives.

Questions:

1. How should you respond to and deal with this committee?
2. What "voice" should a committee like this be allowed to have?
3. How can we achieve a balance between involving parents in their children's education and allowing political groups to adversely influence the school and/or district?
4. How can you find out the real agenda of this committee?

References:

Butler, J.M. et al. 1992. Effective parent involvement strategies as identified by parents, administrators and teachers. ED355027.

Mannan, G., and J. Blackwell. 1992. Parent involvement: Barriers and opportunities. *Urban Review* 24:219-226.

85. FAILURE TO COMPLETE END-OF-YEAR TEACHER EVALUATION

Problem:

It is June. Formal classes are finished for the year. It is final-exam time. There is one teacher on your staff whom you have not formally observed at all this school year. This teacher called in sick the day you had scheduled your formal observation and you were not able to reschedule it. You must fill out an evaluation form on this teacher and he must sign it before he leaves next week.

Background:

Evaluation forms must be completed and signed by the teacher each year. The central office requires that an evaluation form on each member of the staff be sent to them, for filing, at the close of each school year.

Questions:

1. What are the consequences of not conducting a formal observation of a teacher?
2. What is the real problem in this case?
3. What could you do to prevent a similar situation from occurring in the future?
4. How will you resolve this problem?

References:

Airasian, P.W. 1993. Teacher assessment: Some issues for principals. *NASSP Bulletin* 77:55-65

Hartzell, G.N. 1995. Helping administrators learn to avoid seven common employee performance appraisal errors. *Journal of Staff Development* 16:32-37.

Hazard, W.R. 1993. Legal aspects of teacher evaluation. ED377182.

Webster, W. J. 1995. The connection between personnel evaluation and school evaluation. *Studies in Educational Evaluation* 21:227-254.

Wilson, B., and J.A. Wood. 1996. Teacher evaluation: A national dilemma. *Journal of Personnel Evaluation in Education* 10:75-82.

86. GRAFFITI AT RIVAL SCHOOL DURING VARSITY GAME

Problem:

Yesterday, the varsity girls' volleyball team had a game at a neighboring school. Following the volleyball game, someone reported that there was new graffiti on a cafeteria door, and that several decorative posters had been torn down. The graffiti has been traced to two boys who are students from your school. The boys are in trouble academically and socially. (You suspect that there is a substance-abuse problem for both of them.) When confronted about the incident, both boys admitted their involvement.

Background:

The school where the volleyball game took place is your biggest rival, and the two varsity football teams will be playing each other at your school this weekend. Emotions are running high at the other school, and its principal is threatening to press charges. You fear student retaliation before and/or after Saturday's game.

Questions:

1. Since the incident took place off school grounds (and therefore out of your jurisdiction), what can you do?
2. What precautions can you take to prevent a similar incident at your own school?
3. How will you deal with the principal at your rival school?
4. What actions will you take with the two students?

References:

Ferrell, J. 1995. Urban graffiti: Crime, control, and resistance. *Youth and Society* 27:73-92.

Kaufer, S. 1994. Ninety-nine tips for safe schools. ED367060.

Menacker, J., and R. Mertz. 1994. State legislative responses to school crime. *West's Education Law Quarterly* 3:57-65.

Peters, T.C. 1990. Student graffiti and social class: Clues for counselors. *School Counselor* 38:123-132.

Watson, T.S. 1996. A prompt plus delayed contingency procedure for reducing bathroom graffiti. *Journal of Applied Behavior Analysis* 29:121-124.

87. INAPPROPRIATE CHEERLEADER BEHAVIOR

Problem:

A group of high-school soccer cheerleaders devised a vocabulary that would designate which players were popular and which players were not. They incorporated these words into a cheer that takes place at the beginning of every game. Their plan was to use their words at any game where the cheerleading advisor might be late; obviously, they realized that their idea was not acceptable behavior.

Background:

At the soccer game prior to Homecoming, the advisor was detained. Upon her arrival, concerned spectators informed her of the cheerleaders' activities. She immediately decided to suspend them from participating in all Homecoming activities. When the soccer coach was told about the situation, he went one step further. Feeling that the girls were not good representatives for his team, he chose to suspend them from cheering at games for the rest of the season. The girls on the squad were predominantly from upper-middle-class families. They all decided to tell their parents in hopes of gaining support for their side. The next day, a group of ten crying cheerleaders entered your office. Prior to their arrival, most of the parents had called you to say that the punishment was too harsh. Both the girls and parents suggested that you, as principal, overrule the decision of the advisors, and allow them to cheer at Homecoming and all future games.

Questions:

1. What action will you take with the soccer coach and the cheerleading advisor?
2. How will you handle the cheerleaders?
3. What will be your response to the parents?

4. What implications does this situation have regarding all other sports activities at your school?

References:

Lesko, N. 1988. "We're leading America": The changing organization and form of high school cheerleading. *Theory and Research in Social Education* 16:263-278.

Suitor, J.J., and R. Rebel. 1995. Football, fast cars, and cheerleading: Adolescent gender norms, 1978-1989. *Adolescence* 30:265-272.

88. INCOMPETENT SOCIAL-STUDIES TEACHER

Problem:

You, the principal, have just conferred with Mr. Tudor, the social-studies chairperson, about the performance of Mr. Stuart, one of the social-studies teachers. You ended the conference with the following statement to the chairperson: "Henry, we have to do something about Jim Stuart! He has got to improve."

Background:

Mr. Tudor and Mr. Stuart are members of the social-studies department at Hanover High School. Mr. Tudor is chairperson of the department. Mr. Stuart is a tenured and experienced teacher who knows his subject matter. When Mr. Tudor was appointed as chair, Mr. Stuart was his strongest supporter in the department and publicly welcomed the appointment.

Mr. Stuart is no longer a productive classroom teacher. He has become totally disorganized. When Mr. Tudor was observing, he noticed that Mr. Stuart's classes were disorganized, boring, and long-winded. Mr. Stuart wandered from the subject and interjected all sorts of personal anecdotes. Several students and parents have complained to you and demanded to be transferred from his classes. In addition, departmental chores are often neglected and Mr. Stuart's plan book is usually late and often unreadable. Mr. Stuart seems to have no idea of what is going on in his classes. However, he views himself as a vibrant teacher who is meeting the needs of his students.

Questions:

1. In your role as principal, what demands would you make of the department chairperson?
2. How would you get Mr. Stuart to focus on his problems?
3. How does one begin to document a tenured and experienced teacher?
4. How would you handle parent and student complaints?

References:

Bridges, E.M. 1993. The incompetent teacher: Managerial responses. A revised and extended edition. The Stanford series on public policy. ED394176.

Herman, D. 1993. Remediating marginal teachers: What makes plans of assistance work? *OSSC Report* 34:1-12.

Lavely, C. et al. 1992. Actual incidence of incompetent teachers. *Educational Research Quarterly* 15:11-14.

McGrath, M.J. 1993. When it's time to dismiss an incompetent teacher. *School Administrator* 50:30-33.

Waintroob, A.R. 1995. Remediating and dismissing the incompetent teacher. *School Administrator* 52:20-24.

89. LOW PASSING SCORES ON STATEWIDE EXAMS

Problem:

Bob Thompson, tenured high-school math teacher, is being criticized by the administration for his students' low passing rate on statewide math exams. Only 60 percent of his students received a grade of 65 percent or better on the test. Members of the community have become aware of this information and numerous phone calls expressing dismay have been made to you, the high-school principal, and the superintendent of schools.

Background:

Wheaton is a very small district–enrollment is approximately 1,000 students and there are only two buildings in the system. Each time a family leaves the district or puts its children into a private school, loss in enrollment can be expressed in significant percentages. It is important that the district maintain its reputation for good schools so that parents will keep their youngsters in them. Poor showing on statewide exams is against the best interests of this or any other district.

During Mr. Thompson's years of teaching in the district, the administration has viewed him as an uncooperative member of the faculty. A staunch union member, Mr. Thompson has handled grievances for staff during the past several years. He has been belligerent to you and is skeptical about any attempts at positive reinforcement. Mr. Thompson needs to look at new teaching techniques that may improve his test scores.

Questions:

1. What is your plan of action for dealing with Mr. Thompson?
2. What action will you take to improve the scores on the statewide math exam?
3. How will you improve the image of the math program in the eyes of the parents?
4. Whom else should you consult on this matter?

References:

Cuban, L. 1991. The misuse of tests in education. ED340780.

Marso, R.N., and F.L. Pigge. 1992. Classroom teachers' perceptions of the extent and effectiveness of their schools' use of standardized test results. ED342802.

Ornstein, A.C. 1994. Grading practices and policies: An overview and some suggestions. *NASSP Bulletin* 78:55-64.

Swatton, P. 1995. Can we know whether pupils are passing the "fair test"? *Research Papers in Education* 10:51-73.

Whitehead, B., and P. Santee. 1994. Using standardized test results as an instructional guide. *Clearing House* 67:320-322.

90. NAME-CALLING BY SPECIAL-EDUCATION TEACHER

Problem:

A few of the girls in Mr. Harris' special-education class have gone to the assistant principal for the second time to report that Mr. Harris has called them "sluts," "whores," and other derogatory names. You, the principal, spoke to Mr. Harris about these charges, and he denied them. The parents of one of the girls called today to demand a meeting with you. Their daughter had reported the incidents to them and refuses to return to Mr. Harris' class if he continues to call her these names. You are meeting with these parents in three days.

Background:

Mr. Harris is a tenured special-education teacher who has taught special-education students in this school for nineteen years. He currently teaches language arts to fifteen-to twenty-year-old students who spend half the day in occupational training and the other half fulfilling the academic requirements of their program. Mr. Harris is a conservative Baptist raised in North Carolina, where he received a degree in religious education as well as a master's degree. He originally requested to teach elementary-level special-education students, but was assigned to secondary, as that class was open.

During his career at this school, thirteen different administrators have observed Mr. Harris. Noted in each observation were "serious concerns" in the following areas: inadequate lesson planning; poor classroom and behavior management; and little or no program content. Each observation also noted his ability to get along with other staff members and his willingness to volunteer for extra activities.

Questions:

1. What information do you need to obtain to determine if the students' allegations are true?
2. How will you obtain this information?
3. If you determine that Mr. Harris did in fact use derogatory names to the girls, what plan of action will you follow?
4. What will you say to the parents?

References:

Burke, K. 1992. What to do with the kid who.... Developing cooperation, self-discipline, and responsibility in the classroom. K-12. ED370709.

Kearney, P. et al. 1991. What students don't like about what teachers say and do. ED343191.

Kron, L. et al. 1991. An introduction to managing behavior positively. Module 5. ED342165.

Rhone, E. 1992. Improving negative behavior in adolescent pupils through collaborative initiatives. ED346418.

Stensmo, C. 1995. Classroom management styles in context: Two case studies. ED388644.

91. PARENTAL COMPLAINTS ABOUT NEW COURSE

Problem:

You, the principal, have received numerous complaints from parents and students regarding the teacher of a new college-credit course in business administration. Students report that the teacher is making the course boring by his slow speech and by teaching directly from the textbook. The students feel they are learning nothing.

Background:

The teacher, Mr. Patton, has an M.B.A. degree and has had fourteen years of teaching experience. This is his second year at this high school. He received glowing recommendations from his superiors at previous schools. Even though he taught mostly basic-skill courses during his first year in this high school, he seemed to be an excellent teacher. As a result, the department head felt that with his degree he was qualified to teach this course.

Many of the students in the two sections of business administration are in the top academic group in the school. Their parents are actively involved in the parent-teacher association. Obviously, Mr. Patton's methods of teaching (although apparently successful with lower-ability students) do not appeal to the brighter students.

Questions:

1. How should you handle the situation?
2. What factors will influence your decision?
3. What alternatives should you consider?
4. Develop a growth plan for Mr. Patton.

References:

Baumgartner, D. et al. 1993. Thanks for asking: Parent comments about homework, tests, and grades. *Exceptionality: A Research Journal* 4:177-185.

Dike, M.M. 1996. Parental involvement in program expansion: Who knows best? *NHSA Journal* 15:46-47, 49.

Parental involvement: The critical link. 1990. ED387219.

Wagonseller, B.R. 1992. Strategies for developing a positive parent-school partnership. ED349665.

92. PARENTAL USE OF INFLUENCE

Problem:

Ernie Watson, a freshman, was observed smoking pot in the high school by two teachers who submitted both a written and an oral report on the incident. At the end of the day, you, the principal, suspended Ernie from school for a period not to exceed five school days. A suspension letter sent to Ernie's parents indicated that he would be reinstated within the suspension period when a parent met with the assistant principal. Two days later, Mrs. Watson stormed into your office and demanded an immediate conference, even though she did not have an appointment and others were waiting to see you. She demanded to see her son's folder. The folder was not in the files and could not be found anywhere, although it had been used on the day of the suspension. Mrs. Watson accused the teachers of lying and contended that the school "was out to get her son." She demanded an apology from the school for her son's suspension since there was no evidence that he had used pot.

Background:

Ernie has had a long record of behavior problems in the district during the past six years. Each time his mother met with school personnel, she insisted that her son had done nothing wrong. Three years ago Mrs. Watson was hired by a federal program and holds a high position. She has gained much political power within her poverty-stricken neighborhood and has attempted to intimidate school personnel with her newly acquired power and her "connections."

Questions:

1. In this case, the student's folder was misplaced. What is the importance of maintaining a secure system for student records?
2. How will you deal with Mrs. Watson?
3. What should you do to support the teachers?
4. What action can you take to prevent a similar situation from occurring in the future?

5. How will you discipline Ernie?

References:

Educational record and report forms. Annotated bibliography of tests. 1989. ED369802.

Student education records and confidentiality. 1994. ED385941.

Types of contact between parents and school personnel. Indicator of the month. 1996. ED395385.

Yaeger, J.D. 1994. Confidentiality of student records: A guide for school districts establishing policies and procedures with special emphasis on alcohol and other drug use. ED385955.

93. PHYSICAL-EDUCATION CHAIRMAN ABSENTEEISM

Problem:

Mr. Daniels is the chairman of the high-school physical-education department. He has been an employee of the district for fifteen years and has received excellent evaluations. The past two years Mr. Daniels has served as chairman of the department, succeeding a very strong and successful department head. In his two years as department head, he has done nothing to stimulate the program. It has been relatively "status quo" as far as curriculum and he has not implemented anything new. He has also been absent a total of 25 days for the first year and 22 during the second year. Many of those days happened to be on Fridays and Mondays. The physical-education staff has taken note of the excessive absenteeism and has started to talk among themselves. They cite his high number of absences, along with lack of leadership, as the reason for the decline of the physical-education department.

Background:

Mr. Daniels is a certified administrator and is currently working toward a doctorate. He is well respected by the community and administrators, including the athletic director. He serves on the Building Council Committee. The physical-education department was hit hard during the recent budget crisis and lost two full-time positions. Mr. Daniels never spoke to oppose the cuts at budget hearings. The chairman's position is an annual appointment reviewed by the athletic director.

Questions:

1. Should Mr. Daniels be removed? Why or why not?
2. What should be the conditions to keep Mr. Daniels?
3. How should you handle the physical-education staff?
4. What role should the athletic director have in this situation?
5. How will you deal with Mr. Daniels' excessive absences?

References:

Callahan, R.K. 1986. The development and implementation of an absentee improvement program. ED323428.

Evans, W.J., Jr., ed. 1996. Case citations 1996. Eighteenth series (school administrators). ED393189.

Lipoff, Elise. 1991. When illness and disability strike your staff. Here's how. ED328983.

Tips for principals from NASSP, 1981-1989. 1991. ED355630.

94. REFUSAL TO ACCEPT RESPONSIBILITY AS A FACULTY ADVISOR

Problem:

Mr. Benson, social-studies and social-science department head, asks to be excused from serving as faculty advisor. He states that the role just does not suit him and how he relates to the students.

Background:

Mr. Benson is considered the most outstanding teacher in the school. Students fight to get into his classes. He teaches world history, American history and a military history elective. Outside of class, he is very quiet and very proper in the style of an English aristocrat. Rumors abound that he served in the Canadian Military as a noncommissioned officer and in the U.S. Navy aboard submarines. Normal policy requires all teachers to share the load as faculty advisors, receiving some students by choice and some by assignment.

Questions:

1. Should you honor his request not to be an advisor? Why or why not?
2. Are there any other options available for Mr. Benson?

3. Is there a way to have a win/win situation?
4. Should advising be evaluated, just as teaching is evaluated? Why or why not?

References:

Bushnell, D., and P.S. George. 1993. Five crucial characteristics: Middle school teachers as effective advisers. *Schools in the Middle* 3:10-16.

George, P.S., and D. Bushnell. 1993. What works and why? The key to successful advisement activities. *Schools in the Middle* 3:3-9.

Granese, J. 1992. How to be a great club adviser. ED356199.

Laird, J. 1995. Survival guide for class and club advisers. ED382912.

Witmer, J.T. 1992. Teachers as advisers. *Executive Educator* 14:41-42.

95. SECURITY AT THE JUNIOR PROM

Problem:

It is Monday afternoon following the junior prom. You have just received a call from the superintendent, who asks you, the principal, to explain events that occurred at the prom last Friday night. The prom was held at a very upscale hotel. He received a call from the PTA president who had heard "through the grapevine" that parties involving alcohol were held in private rooms during the dance. The superintendent also heard that the "faculty table" in the ballroom was served alcohol. In addition, it was reported to him that hotel rooms were rented by students with the prior knowledge of high-school staff and parents. Millburn students who did not attend the prom were seen entering the hotel after midnight, when the dance ended, and getting on elevators to go to hotel rooms.

Background:

The hotel management assured Mr. Jackson, the class advisor, that security at the junior prom would be "tight." Front-desk personnel were alerted to be diligent in asking for identification and proof of age for those suspected of being underage.

Upon learning that a party was taking place on the fifth floor, Mr. Jackson and a fellow teacher alerted hotel security. When they received no satisfactory response, they spent two hours tracking and investigating students who left the ballroom, and with the eventual help of a security person, "busted the room."

This morning Mr. Jackson gained access to the hotel computer records through the hotel manager and discovered that a total of eight rooms were rented to students on the evening of the junior prom.

Questions:

1. How will you determine exactly what happened on Friday night?
2. What actions will you take with the students?
3. How will you handle the teachers who were chaperoning the prom?
4. If you find that the faculty was drinking alcohol during the prom, what action will you take?
5. What, if any, actions will you take with the hotel?

References:

Gittins, N., ed. 1990. School law in review, 1990: Presentations from the annual School Law Seminar. ED321399.

Murphy, S.C. 1994. Celebrate life! A guide for planning all-night alcohol/drug-free celebrations for teens. Fifth edition. ED388925.

96. STOLEN FINAL EXAM

Problem:

The French final exam was stolen during the final weeks of school, when everyone in the high school was busy with finals and classroom cleaning. The French teachers did not realize that the exam and a faculty member's answer keys had been stolen until virtually everyone in the class received a perfect score on the test. The teachers were able to remember where the keys to the storage closet containing the foreign-language exams had been left. They also remembered the student who had last been seen in the department office. You, the principal, called this student into your office, and he confessed to taking the exam and answer key. However, several other students had been in on the cheating, although not directly involved with the theft. Many of these students were honors-level juniors and seniors and members of the National Honor Society.

Parents of some of these students are very concerned about the possible effects of this incident on college acceptances and references.

You are being pressured to drop the charges as well as the consequences. One parent has taken the matter to his lawyer.

Background:

Putnam High School recently received a Blue Ribbon Award for Excellence from the federal government. The district is affluent and conservative. More than 90 percent of the high-school graduates go on to college. When anything goes wrong, there is rarely any "leak" to the public; the faculty is often not informed of the problem either.

Questions:

1. What punishment will you administer to the student who stole the exam and answer keys?
2. How will you deal with the students who participated in the "cheating" incident?
3. How will you respond to the parents' demands and threats?
4. How will you safeguard all exams in the future?
5. What school policies, if any, will you amend, in order to prevent this type of problem in the future?

References:

Mehrens, W.A. et al. 1993. Survey of test security practices. *Educational Measurement: Issues and Practice* 12:5-9, 19.

Van Dyke, J.M., and M.M. Sakurai. 1992. Checklists for searches and seizures in public schools. ED352705.

Wiggins, G. 1994. The immortality of test security. *Educational Policy* 8:157-182.

97. STUDENT ABSENCE FOR ABORTION

Problem:

You are a high-school principal in a state that requires parental consent for a minor to have a legal abortion. You have just been told that one of your students has arranged to have an abortion without parent or court approval. Her parents are divorced and she is in the custody of her mother, Mrs. Jones. Her father is a lawyer, who is remarried and living in Chicago. Your working relationship with the mother has been poor. She is a heavy drinker (possibly alcoholic), calls the school often demanding that her daughter be taken from class to talk with her, provides fraudulent written excuses and is of the opinion that her daughter's actions and words are beyond reproach.

Background:

Afternoon attendance reveals that Sue Jones and Carol Brown are absent from school. They were together in the lunchroom, which leads you to believe they might be skipping school. You choose not to call Mrs. Jones due to her past negative reactions to such calls. In fact, she has made it clear that she always knows where her daughter is, does not appreciate your detective work, and recommends you pay more attention to troublemakers.

A phone call to Mrs. Brown reveals that Carol is skipping school. Within the hour, Mrs. Brown calls back to let you know that Carol is on her way to your office and that you are to discipline her as you see fit. While talking with Carol you learn that she and Sue had gone to a large neighboring town after lunch to arrange an abortion for Sue. Carol relates that Sue is in dread of her mother learning of this, and the mere mention of it evokes hysterical reactions on her part. The abortion is to be performed in the doctor's office tomorrow at 10:30 a.m.

At 9:00 a.m. the following morning, Mr. and Mrs. Brown come to your office to discuss their daughter's skipping school. They soon let you know that Carol related the complete situation concerning Sue to them. The Browns assisted their daughter in having an abortion last year and realize you are aware of this. Your secretary notes that Sue is not in her second-period class today although she was in school at 8:30 a.m.

Questions:

1. How do you handle the immediate situation regarding Sue?
2. How do you proceed with the Browns?
3. How do you deal with Mrs. Jones?
4. What steps do you take with Carol?
5. With whom in the district do you consult in this matter?

References:

Calhoun, S.W. 1995. Impartiality in the classroom: A personal account of a struggle to be evenhanded in teaching about abortion. *Journal of Legal Education* 45:99-112.

Hardy, J.B., and L.S. Zabin. 1991. Adolescent pregnancy in an urban environment: Issues, programs, and evaluation. ED362621.

Hughes, T. 1994. Everything you need to know about teen pregnancy. Revised edition. The need to know library. ED385815.

Santelli, J.S. et al. 1992. Adolescent sexuality: Pregnancy, sexually transmitted diseases, and prevention. *Journal of School Health* 62:255-361.

Stolley, K.S., and E.J. Hall. 1994. The presentation of abortion and adoption in marriage and family textbooks. *Family Relations* 43:267-273.

98. STUDENT ATHLETES DRINKING

Problem:

Each year all football players sign a contract pledging not to drink alcohol or smoke during the football season. This fall a group of football players, among other students, became involved with the police when someone got hurt at a Saturday-night party. The police determined that many of the players were "under the influence." The coach informed the football players that they would be ineligible to play in the next game because they broke their contract. The team had to forfeit the game because there were not enough players.

Different groups in the school and the community had differing opinions. Most teachers felt that the coach did the right thing. Several parents felt that there was inequity because other students caught drinking played on other teams that also had contracts, and the coaches of those teams had not punished their players. Others questioned the legality of the contract. Some community groups were very upset about forfeiting a game. A group of parents and community members have asked for a meeting with you to resolve this problem.

Background:

Merrill High School is located in a small, affluent school district. The secondary schools have highly successful teams, many of which win championships. The community generously supports sports. There is a booster club made up of local businessmen that contributes to the teams on a regular basis.

Questions:

1. Will you support the actions taken by the football coach? Why or why not?
2. How will you deal with the parents' charge of unfair treatment of some students?
3. How will you deal with the community groups that are upset about what has happened?
4. What should you, the principal, do when you feel that "contract" agreements are inequitably enforced?
5. What evidence would the police have to present to support their claim that these students were drinking?

References:

Carr, C.N. et al. 1990. Alcohol use among high school athletes: A comparison of alcohol use and intoxication in male and female high school athletes and non-athletes. *Journal of Alcohol and Drug Education* 36:39-43.

Jerry-Szpak, J., and H.P. Brown, Jr. 1994. Alcohol use and misuse: The hidden curriculum of the adolescent athlete. *Journal of Child and Adolescent Substance Abuse* 3:57-68.

Ringwalt, C. 1988. Student athletes and non-athletes: Do their use of and beliefs about alcohol and other drugs differ? Special Research Report. ED300751.

99. SUSPENSION OF SPECIAL-EDUCATION STUDENTS

Problem:

You are the supervisor of an eleven-class special–education program for high–school–age special–education students. One of your staff, Mr. Smith, has given you a proposal that would help alleviate the growing number of teacher-requested suspensions. After some discussion with Mr. Smith, you suggest that the proposal be brought up and discussed at next week's staff meeting. At the meeting, Mr. Smith's proposal is panned. The other staff members are very negative toward it, even somewhat threatened as to the implication for change in their approach to discipline. After a brief and slightly heated discussion, other staff business is discussed with no further discussion of the planned proposal. As supervisor, you appreciate the concern and effort demonstrated by Mr. Smith's proposal and agree upon the importance of its implementation, but you, too, realize the difficulty of effecting change on this issue without staff support.

Background:

The eleven classes are located in seven different school districts in the county. This makes uniformity of action a constant problem. The staff see very little of one another except at monthly staff meetings. The special-education students require special procedures for their education in general and alternative approaches with regard to discipline in particular.

Questions:

1. What techniques can be employed by the supervisor to gain support of the proposal?
2. How does one retain Mr. Smith's enthusiasm after such rejection?
3. How can future "pannings" of proposals be avoided?

References:

Busick, K.U. et al. 1994. Synthesis of the research on educational change. ED376599.

Gainey, D.D. 1994. The American high school and change: An unsettling process. *NASSP Bulletin* 78:26-34.

Glickman, C.D. et al. 1994. Factors affecting school change. *Journal of Staff Development* 15:37-41.

Macon, L., ed. 1991. Learning disabilities in the high school: A methods booklet for secondary special subject teachers. ED363048.

Maeroff, G.I. 1993. Team building for school change: Equipping teachers for new roles. ED360707.

100. TEACHER'S ABUSIVE BEHAVIOR

Problem:

Over the past year, there has been a marked change in Mr. Cleaver's personality, which has caused great concern on the part of the faculty. He has become extremely vindictive and abusive; he uses inappropriate language, such as calling the children, "little twits", "nerds", and "bastards." He has a baseball bat in his room that he uses to hit desks and chairs. He also insults the children's lifestyles to such a degree that some parents have complained.

Background:

Mr. Cleaver is a tenured English teacher who has been teaching at Jackson High School for twenty years. Over the years, he has earned a reputation of being an excellent teacher and he continues to be one of the most creative and innovative teachers on the staff. His students read the most advanced literature and perform exceptionally well on the final examination. Mr. Cleaver has also been very active in student counseling, and has had the reputation among the students as a teacher you can trust and a person who is always willing to fight for you. He is well respected among the faculty for his intelligence, wit, and insight. At faculty meetings, he comes up with original ideas and follows through with every task. However, during this year, he has gone through two very stressful events: heart surgery and a messy divorce.

Questions:

1. What can you, the principal, do to provide assistance to Mr. Cleaver?
2. Devise a step-by-step plan for improvement for Mr. Cleaver. Include whom you would involve, what resources you would use, and what timeline you would follow.
3. What would you say to Mr. Cleaver?
4. How do you respond to parent complaints?
5. How will you deal with faculty concerns?

References:

Frame, D. 1996. Maslow's hierarchy of needs revisited. *Interchange* 27:13-22.

Martin, N.K. et al. 1995. Beliefs regarding classroom management style: Relationships to particular teacher personality characteristics. ED387461.

Rich, S.J. 1995. Teacher support groups: Why they emerge and the role they play. *Education Canada* 35:15-21.

Sheperd, M.F., and J.A. Campbell. 1992. The Abusive Behavior Inventory: A measure of psychological and physical abuse. *Journal of Interpersonal Violence* 7:291-305.

101. TEACHER ACCUSED OF HITTING STUDENT

Problem:

Several years ago a male high-school student became enraged by Mr. Stanley's unyielding manner and accused him of hitting and pushing him. There weren't any witnesses to this alleged incident. After a full hearing, the teacher was exonerated, mostly due to a lack of evidence presented in the student's testimony. Recently the same teacher and a female student became involved in a similar incident. This time, there were many witnesses present. This student and her parents have come to you, the principal, and demanded that the teacher be fired. They have hired an attorney. The teacher stated that he never hit the student. He says he only assisted her to the door, by holding her elbow, after she refused to leave the room. The students who witnessed the incident are backing the student.

Background:

Mr. Stanley is a science teacher who has been the director of the high-school planetarium for many years. He only teaches two classes each day. The rest of the day is reserved for him to schedule visits to the planetarium for school grades one through eight, where he presents a variety of programs. He does a great job and his programs are well received. He has a formal, rigid, dry personality that causes many of the students and staff to react to him in a negative way. His standoffish, confrontational attitude has created more than one serious problem.

Questions:

1. As principal, you must resolve this case. How can you determine what really happened?
2. Whom will you use as sources of information?
3. How will you deal with Mr. Stanley?
4. How will you deal with the students?
5. What actions will you take with the female student's parents?
6. What legal implications are there in this situation?

References:

Davis, P.W. 1996. Threats of corporal punishment as verbal aggression: A naturalistic study. *Child Abuse and Neglect: The International Journal* 20:289-304.

Doverspike, D.E., and W.H. Cone. 1992. The principal and the law. Elementary principal series. No. 7. ED355647.

Evans, E.D., and R.C. Richardson. 1995. Corporal punishment: What teachers should know. *Teaching Exceptional Children* 27:33-36.

Hyman, R.T., and C.H. Rathbone. 1993. The principal's decision: A teaching monograph on corporal punishment. NOLPE monograph series, No. 48A. ED357448.

Sachs, J.J. et al. 1992. Administration of corporal punishment: Where are the procedural safeguards? *Education* 113:312-318.

102. TEACHER ASSAULT OF STUDENT

Problem:

For several months Mr. Robbins has been having difficulty with a sophomore who has been harassing him. Mr. Robbins is six feet, two inches, and the student is just over five feet tall. Two days ago the student elbowed Mr. Robbins in the ribs as he was walking into his class. After about ten minutes, Mr. Robbins called the security guard and sat down to write up the incident. When the student realized what the teacher was doing, he began to taunt the teacher. Mr. Robbins spun around in an irate stance, kicked the student, hit him in the face and threw him to the floor. The incident was witnessed by the security guard. Mr. Robbins wrote up the entire sequence of events. You called Mr. Robbins into your office and asked if he wanted representation. Mr. Robbins refused and gave you the written documentation of the events. The student was suspended and the parents are suing the teacher.

Background:

Mr. Robbins is a high-school math teacher. He has been teaching seven years but just received tenure last year. By his own admission, he failed the math-licensing exam but argued his case with the board and passed the test. He has been in his present school two years. This is the third school in which he has taught.

With colleagues, Mr. Robbins' attitude is one of superiority. With students, he projects a macho, tough-guy image. He is an assistant coach of the basketball team but refers to himself as the coach. All of his students failed last year's statewide math test.

Mr. Robbins has a black belt in karate and is an active member of the NAACP. The math-department chairman has complained to you about Mr. Robbins' ineffectiveness in class as well as his stern treatment of students. There are currently four legal suits against the school district from various employees, all involving discrimination.

Questions:

1. What disciplinary action should be taken against Mr. Robbins for hitting a student?
2. What further action should be taken against the student?
3. How will you deal with the parents?
4. What role will you play in the parents' lawsuit against the teacher?
5. With whom should you consult concerning this many-faceted problem, which includes student rights, due process, possible allegations of racial discrimination, public relations issues, etc.?

References:

Butt, K.L., and M.L. Pahnos. 1995. Why we need a multicultural focus in our schools. *Journal of Physical Education, Recreation and Dance* 66:48-53.

Greenlee, A.R., and E.J. Ogletree. 1993. Teachers' attitudes toward student discipline problems and classroom management strategies. ED364330.

Mendler, A.N. 1992. What do I do when? How to achieve discipline with dignity in the classroom. ED357109.

Tobin, J., and R.A. Johnson. 1994. A multicultural, multivocal, multimedia approach to teaching classroom management and preservice teachers. *Teaching Education* 6:113-122.

VanOostendorp, K.D. 1991. Effect of student gender bias toward the instructor on classroom management at the secondary level. ED346191.

103. TEACHER BURNOUT

Problem:

Mrs. Ashe received tenure as a social-studies teacher at Fair Acres High School before Ms. Stoker became department chairperson. Ms.

Stoker has found Mrs. Ashe to be not only "burned-out" but inept as well. She feels that Mrs. Ashe has taught one year, twenty times over. Not only are her daily study-guide questions the same year after year, but they are barely legible since they have been copied so many times. She has even stooped so low as to make copies of her old planbook and staple the pages into her current one. Ms. Stoker also notes that Mrs. Ashe is using instruction that does not involve interaction with students. During one observation, Mrs. Ashe conducted most of the lesson facing the blackboard. Last year, Ms. Stoker suggested that Mrs. Ashe find ways to share notes and information without having to turn her back to the students. That year the department was issued three overhead projectors and one was given to Mrs. Ashe. She now teaches using only the overhead.

Background:

Ms. Stoker decided that a change in program might light a fire under Mrs. Ashe. She therefore assigned her new and more challenging classes to teach this year. The former principal changed this assignment and gave Mrs. Ashe the lowest-level classes possible. These classes are small and parent involvement is minimal. A teacher can get away without doing much. On the other hand, these students are among the most difficult to motivate and the most needy of strong teacher involvement. As the new principal, you are faced with the decision of keeping Mrs. Ashe with the low classes she has been assigned or transferring her back to the level of students she has worked with in the past. You only have three weeks before school begins.

Questions:

1. Should you take Mrs. Ashe's wishes into consideration when considering this assignment?
2. How should you involve Ms. Stokes in your decision-making process?
3. What are the pros and cons of leaving Mrs. Ashe with the lower-functioning students? Of moving her to work with the regular classes?
4. What recommendations for improvement would you make to Mrs. Ashe?
5. What assistance would you give her?

References:

Berg, B.D. 1994. Educator burnout revisited: Voices from the staff room. *Clearing House* 67:185-188.

Byrne, B.M. 1994. Testing for the validity, replication, and invariance of causal structure across elementary, intermediate, and secondary teachers. *American Educational Research Journal* 31:645-673.

Canter, L. 1994. The high-performing teacher. ED380460.

Friedman, I.A., and B.A. Farber. 1992. Professional self-concept as a predictor of teacher burnout. *Journal of Educational Research* 86:28-35.

Littrell, P.C. et al. 1994. The effects of principal support on special and general educators' stress, job satisfaction, school commitment, health, and intent to stay in teaching. *Remedial and Special Education* 15:297-310.

104. TEACHER'S ERRATIC BEHAVIOR

Problem:

Mr. Richards teaches social studies in the high school. During the last school year, his attendance and behavior in school became erratic. By December, he had suffered a complete nervous breakdown and was hospitalized. After using all his sick days, he applied to the union's "sick bank" and was granted enough additional leave to permit him time off for the remainder of the school year. Mr. Richards returned to his regular assignment this past September, only to begin, almost immediately, his erratic behavior. This generally consisted of lateness to class, forgetfulness, inconsistent disciplinary techniques with students, and inability to relate to other staff members. His dress was likewise unconventional and inappropriate. After being spoken to by several administrators and peers, he again applied for some time off from the sick bank. He was granted several days, but they quickly ran out and the teachers' association became reluctant to give him more time because it did not appear that he was trying to rehabilitate himself. He returned to work after Christmas vacation and was given nonteaching duties to perform for the rest of the school year. His behavior has changed very little in the meantime.

Background:

Mr. Richards was married to a young English teacher in the same school district. They had taught together in the high school for nine years when she left him to live with the married father of one of her students. Needless to say, this caused grief not only for her husband but for almost everyone else involved (the community had a field day with the ensuing gossip). This event seemed to be the catalyst for the nervous breakdown. In fact, on weekends, Mr. Richards often follows his ex-wife when she leaves the house (she and the married man live in the district). The union and the administration have been sympathetic to the man's extraordinary situation, but will soon be entering a new school year with the assumption that nothing much has changed. A number of parents have complained, and many have requested that their children not be placed in Mr. Richards' classes.

Questions:

1. What documentation should you have on Mr. Richards?
2. What assistance should you expect from the district office in dealing with Mr. Richards?
3. What action should you take?
4. If you decide to put Mr. Richards back in the classroom, how will you deal with the parents?

References:

Dworkin, A.G. et al. 1990. Stress and illness behavior among urban public school teachers. *Educational Administration Quarterly* 26:60-72.

Lawrence, C.E. et al. 1993. The marginal teacher: A step-by-step guide to fair procedures for identification and dismissal. ED358568.

Madden, H.D. et al. 1991. Teacher absences: Are there implications for educational restructuring? ED343199.

Saks, A.L., and R.L. Larson. 1996. Annotated bibliography of research in the teaching of English. *Research in the Teaching of English* 30:248-275.

Scott, K.D., and J.C. Wimbush. 1991. Teacher absenteeism in secondary education. *Educational Administration Quarterly* 27:506-529.

105. TEACHER HOMOSEXUALITY

Problem:

The parents of one student have requested to you and the superintendent that their son be transferred to a different class because the teacher, Mr. Laine, allegedly made inappropriate remarks in class concerning his homosexual experiences and homosexuality in general. Overall, the main complaint centers on Mr. Laine's "abrasive" teaching style and his frequent discussions, with classes, of controversial issues not always related to any particular class topic.

Background:

Mr. Laine has taught high-school English for fifteen years in Elting High School. His professional record has been unblemished throughout this time, although numerous complaints by students and some parents have recently arisen.

Questions:

1. What action would you take with Mr. Laine?
2. How can you, as principal, get at the facts in this case?
3. How will you respond to the parent request for transfer?
4. What should be done to avoid this type of problem in the future?

References:

Harbeck, K.M., ed. 1992. Coming out of the classroom closet: Gay and lesbian students, teachers, and curricula. ED397002.

Juul, T.P. 1996. Joining gay and lesbian teacher organizations: A study of members and non-members. ED397022.

Juul, T.P. 1994. Tenure, civil rights laws, inclusive contracts, and fear: Legal protection and the lives of self-identified lesbian, gay male and bisexual public school teachers. ED377565.

Mayer, M. 1990. Gay, lesbian, and heterosexual teachers: Acceptance of self, acceptance of others, affectional and lifestyle orientation. ED347164.

106. TEACHER IMPOSITION OF PRO-CHOICE ATTITUDE

Problem:

A number of students have come to you, the principal, voicing displeasure about their biology teacher's reference to abortion as murder and that "pro-choice is no choice." They also tell you that he has informed students that he will award extra credit to any student who joins him on Saturday mornings in front of the local Women's Health Clinic to picket the "butchering of babies."

You have just driven past the clinic after grocery shopping and see Dr. Ryan, the biology teacher, with a group of students carrying signs with pro-life slogans.

Background:

Dr. Ryan is the chairman of your high school's science department. His biology course includes a six-week unit on sexual reproduction and health. Dr. Ryan has been a teacher in the school system and a member of the community for thirty-seven years. He enjoys an easy rapport with the faculty and the students.

Questions:

1. Does Dr. Ryan have the right to voice his "pro-choice" opinion to his tenth-grade classes?
2. What actions would you take regarding Dr. Ryan's urging his students to picket in front of the abortion clinic?
3. How will you handle the "extra credit" problem?
4. How will you prevent other teachers from "indoctrinating" their students with their own moral and political positions?

References:

Berne, L.A., and B.K. Huberman. 1995. Sexuality education: Sorting fact from fiction. *Phi Delta Kappan* 77:229-232.

Calhoun, S.W. 1995. Impartiality in the classroom: A personal account of a struggle to be evenhanded in teaching about abortion. *Journal of Legal Education* 45:99-112.

Greene, E. 1995. Teaching about psychological perspectives on abortion. *Teaching of Psychology* 22:202-204.

Press, A.L., and E.R. Cole. 1995. Reconciling faith and fact: Pro-life women discuss media, science and the abortion debate. *Critical Issues in Mass Communication* 12:380-402.

Sullivan, P.A., and S.R. Goldzwig. 1995. A relational approach to moral decision-making: The majority opinion in "Planned Parenthood v. Casey." *Quarterly Journal of Speech* 81:167-190.

107. TEACHER PRACTICING LAW DURING SCHOOL TIME

Problem:

For the past twelve years Dr. Grant has had very poor results when his teaching assignment has included advanced-level courses. In addition, his absentee rate has been very high. As a result there have been increasing numbers of complaints from parents of students in his advanced-level classes. Because of this situation, the central office has made a verbal request that he not be assigned advanced courses whenever possible. Since receiving his law degree he has begun to use school time to proceed with his law practice; he takes time off to study for his bar exams and makes and receives phone calls from clients and other lawyers openly in front of his colleagues. As a result of these factors Dr. Grant's relationship with colleagues has been compromised and his behavior has had a very significant effect on both his colleagues and the students.

Background:

Dr. Grant is a tenured high-school science teacher. In addition to science certification (general science, chemistry, earth science, and physics) he also holds certification in English and industrial arts. For the first three to five years, in addition to his teaching duties, he was student-council advisor and active in state-affiliated student government groups. At that time, he began his studies for a doctorate in education. Upon receiving his doctorate, he unsuccessfully applied for several administrative positions in the district, including elementary-school principal, middle-school principal, and science-department chairman. He then entered law school, completed his studies, and received a law degree. Dr. Grant prepared for and took the bar exam in four states while continuing his full-time assignment as a classroom science teacher.

Questions:

1. As principal of the school, what action should you take regarding Dr. Grant?
2. List the problems in this case study in order of most critical to least critical.
3. Develop specific plans to deal with each problem cited in question two.

References:

Bitner, T., and R. Kratzner. 1995. A primer on building teacher evaluation instruments. ED394953.

Ellett, C.D. et al. 1996. Looking backwards with the "Personnel Evaluation Standards": An analysis of the development and implementation of a statewide teacher assessment program. *Studies in Educational Evaluation* 22:79-113.

Machell, J. 1995. The teacher evaluation environment: An examination of attributes related to teacher growth. *Journal of Personnel Evaluation in Education* 9:259-273.

McColskey, W., and P. Egelson. 1993. Designing teacher evaluation systems that support professional growth. ED367662.

Peterson, K.D. 1995. Teacher evaluation: A comprehensive guide to new directions and practices. ED386825.

108. TEACHER RACISM

Problem:

Mrs. Brown, a high-school English teacher, has a duty period located outside the cafeteria in the main building. Two days ago, she reported that there was a group of minority males outside the cafeteria sitting on the bench abusing a handicapped student who was standing next to them. She said that they were unduly cruel and mean. Mrs. Brown stated that she could not stand there and continue to let this behavior on the part of the minority students go unchecked. She took them to the office and demanded that they be severely punished. The boys reported that Mrs. Brown overreacted and got involved in something that she didn't quite understand. They said she made the following statements to them: "Why don't you stop acting your color?"; "You're animals and should be locked up." Yesterday, parents of the minority students appeared in your office. They demanded that strong action be taken against Mrs. Brown for her insulting and racist remarks and that she apologize to their children. They threatened to take this matter to the board of education and elsewhere if necessary.

Background:

Mrs. Brown, an innovative, dedicated and meticulous English teacher, works diligently at teaching her students. Her apparent success in preparing students for college is well known by her colleagues. She is a well-respected member of the English department. She also does a great deal of voluntary community work. There had been concern by the former principal regarding her past dealings with minority students.

Questions:

1. How can you find out what really happened in this situation? Whom do you need to consult?
2. How should you deal with Mrs. Brown?
3. What actions do you take with the students?
4. What responses will you give to the parents who are so upset?
5. How can you improve the treatment of handicapped students by regular students?

References:

Boutte, G.S., and B. McCoy. 1994. Racial issues in education: Real or imagined? ED376945.

Cross, B.E. 1993. How do we prepare teachers to improve race relations? *Educational Leadership* 50:64-65.

Hall, J.L. 1993. What can we expect from minority students? *Contemporary Education* 64:180-182.

Kailin, J. 1994. Anti-racist staff development for teachers: Considerations of race, class, and gender. *Teaching and Teacher Education* 10:169-184.

Short, G. 1992. Responding to racism in prospective teachers. *Journal of Education for Teaching* 18:173-183.

109. TEACHER REFUSAL TO SIGN CLASSROOM OBSERVATION REPORT

Problem:

The new high-school assistant principal observed Mr. Lemon in a basic mathematics class. The class was very unruly. The students called out inappropriate comments and deliberately gave wrong answers to problems. The observation listed three future objectives pertaining to classroom management and control, as well as homework checks for student accountability. During the postobservation meeting with the assistant principal and you, the principal, Mr. Lemon became agitated when discussing the three future objectives. He felt that with a low-level course such as this one, any response is better than none from his students. He also commented on the content of the observation as being something out of "Supervision 101." He would not sign the observation and promised a written response to challenge future objectives stated by the administrator. Three weeks have passed and you still have not received a written response from Mr. Lemon.

Background:

Mr. Lemon is a tenured mathematics teacher with over twenty years' experience in the school district. During that time, Mr. Lemon has taught the highest-level courses given. Recently, Mr. Lemon has been teaching the lowest-level classes as well as a couple of computer classes. He has also been given a decreasing student load year after year. His abrasive attitude and short fuse with the students also cause some of them to drop his courses.

Questions:

1. As the new high-school principal, what further information do you need to obtain about Mr. Lemon's teaching?
2. What motivational techniques can you use to improve Mr. Lemon's attitude and classroom management skills?
3. If Mr. Lemon's instructional and behavioral management techniques do not improve, what course of action will you take?

References:

Brown, J.L. 1995. Observing dimensions of learning in classrooms and schools. ED390166.

Sikorski, M.F. et al. 1994. Best teaching practices: A checklist for observations. *NASSP Bulletin* 78:50-54.

Struyk, L.R. 1991. Self-evaluation procedures for teachers. ED336361.

Taylor, J.C., and R. G. Romanczyk. 1994. Generating hypotheses about the function of student problem behavior by observing teacher behavior. *Journal of Applied Behavior Analysis* 27:251-265.

Wheeler, P. 1992. Improving classroom observation skills: Guidelines for teacher evaluation. ED364961.

110. TEACHER REQUEST FOR PREFERENTIAL SCHEDULE

Problem:

Mr. Phillips has asked Mrs. Lombard, the department chair, for period one as a preparation period for next year. Mr. Phillips made a similar request two years ago claiming that he lives far away and occasionally might be late due to weather. He then proceeded to cut first period every day. When questioned by Mrs. Lombard, he claimed to have the former principal's permission to arrive late. When Mrs. Lombard went to the former principal to ask if he sanctioned this situation, she was told she had to develop an extra job for him to do after school to make up the time. Mr. Phillips did not complete the assigned job and left school at the regular time. Mrs. Lombard is opposed to creating another situation like the one that occurred previously and has come to you, the new principal, for support.

Background:

Mr. Phillips has seniority in the department. He was passed over for the department chair and Mrs. Lombard was appointed. Mr. Phillips has since expressed his displeasure in a series of insubordinate problem behaviors. No one wants to deal with the scenes he creates. You took over as principal in January and agree that Mr. Phillips should not receive preferential treatment in terms of his schedule.

Questions:

1. How will you handle Mr. Phillips if he creates a scene when you inform him he cannot have period one as a preparation period every day?
2. What types of support will you provide to the department chair when Mr. Phillips blames her for coming to you?
3. How can administrators insure that all staff members receive fair and equitable treatment?

References:

Campbell, R.J., and S.R. Neill. 1991. The workloads of secondary school teachers. ED358042.

Campbell, R.J., and S.R. Neill. 1992. The use and management of secondary teachers' time after the Education Reform Act 1988. ED358044.

How much time do public and private school teachers spend in their work? 1994. ED377550.

Young, B., and K. Grieve. 1996. Negotiating time: Reduced work employment arrangements for teachers. ED397512.

111. TEACHER/STUDENT AFFAIR

Problem:

Smithville High School graduation is three weeks away. As strange as it may seem, Julie Berkely, a member of the senior class, comes to you, the principal, and tells you that she plans to invite Mr. Peterson, one of her teachers, "as a guest" to the senior prom. She requests your approval. She tells you that Mr. Peterson is a member of the senior-class advisory group and will be at the prom anyway. She further states that her mother approves and has encouraged her to come to you with this request.

After Julie leaves, you call Mrs. Berkely to discuss the situation and she supports Julie's request. In addition, she advises you against interfering with her daughter's social life.

Background:

Mr. Peterson is one of the young superstar social-studies teachers at your school. He just received tenure at the April board meeting. He is an outstanding coach, and Julie's brother is one of his star players. When Mr. Peterson's new bride walked out on him last year, both faculty and students were devastated. Mr. and Mrs. Berkely, who are very fond of Mr. Peterson, took him under their wing. They frequently had him as a dinner guest and included him in several family outings. It was during this time that he and Julie developed a relationship. It had been rumored that they were seen together in a neighboring city, but you thought nothing of it since you knew he was close to the family.

Questions:

1. How do you respond to Julie's request?
2. Julie's mother has presented you with a veiled threat. How do you respond to her?
3. What action do you take with Mr. Peterson?
4. How do you deal with the gossip that is circulating among the students?

References:

Hustoles, T.P., and C.A. Duerr, Jr. 1994. Dealing with employee misconduct on and off duty: A practical framework. *CUPA Journal* 45:1-10.

Valente, W.D. 1992. Liability for teachers' sexual misconduct with students—closing and opening vistas. *West's Education Law Quarterly* 1:284-295.

Wilson, R. 1994. Strained relations at Penn. *Chronicle of Higher Education* 41:31-32.

112. TEACHERS' UNION COMPLAINTS ABOUT SUPERVISORY PRACTICES

Problem:

The teachers' union published an unsigned letter in its information bulletin to teachers that criticized one of your supervisors for various practices. The criticisms were enumerated as follows.

1. Stops into classrooms without letting the teacher know, stays from twenty minutes to half the teaching day, and then reports to the teacher his written observation.
2. Writes an evaluation on all aspects of the teacher and classroom, without having spent time there for years.
3. Writes mainly critical evaluations and has no follow-through. He does not offer concrete suggestions as to how a teacher might improve, nor does he help a teacher improve once he has made a critical statement.
4. Opens teacher's desk drawers when the teacher is not in the room. This has been reported by aides and substitute teachers.
5. Looks into teachers' files while the teacher is away. This has been noted by substitute teachers.
6. Stated to a teacher that a child was scheduled for removal to a special school, but held the teacher responsible for that child's behavior until the move was made.
7. Writes threatening letters with critical remarks to teachers, but does not help those teachers in any way.

Background:

This is your first year as principal of Melbourne High School. The supervisor under attack has been a subject supervisor for seven years. He is considered "pro-administration" by the union leaders. You have a reputation of demanding a high level of excellence from your teaching and supervisory staff, which has begun to cause some concerns to the union membership.

Questions:

1. What, if anything, should you do in response to the letter?
2. How do you determine whether the allegations are true?
3. If any of the allegations are true, how should you respond?
4. If any of the allegations are not true, should you respond?
5. Whom should you consult regarding this problem?
6. What actions will you take with the supervisor?

References:

Glanz, J. 1996. Pedagogical correctness in teacher education: Discourse about the role of supervision. ED397058.

Greene, M.L. 1992. Teacher supervision as professional development: Does it work? *Journal of Curriculum and Supervision* 7:131-148.

Hazi, H.M. 1994. The teacher evaluation-supervision dilemma: A case of entanglements and irreconcilable differences. *Journal of Curriculum and Supervision* 9:195-216.

Jones, N.B. 1995. Professional development through democratic supervision. ED389209.

Riordan, G.P. 1995. Teachers' perceptions of collaboration and clinical supervision. ED385494.

113. TEENAGE PREGNANCY

Problem:

Jane Lattes, a high-school sophomore, denies that she is pregnant. Her behavior has been highly volatile and she has been absent several days within the past month. She frequently runs out of the classroom to the bathroom; when questioned, she tells the teacher she has a stomach virus. Two of Jane's closest friends have come to you, the principal, to tell you that they are very worried that she is so sick. They tell you that she is two months' pregnant and that she has sworn them to secrecy.

Background:

You asked Jane's mother to come to school to discuss Jane's recent absences and behavior. When she appeared with Jane, she produced a letter from the Planned Parenthood clinic indicating that someone who had been tested for pregnancy had used her older daughter's name. The test results were positive. When asked, the mother assured you that her older daughter was not pregnant. When questioned, Jane assured you and her mother that she was not pregnant either, but rather it was one of the other girls in her class who has used Jane's sister's name. The other girl Jane accused of being pregnant has not been absent one day, is always in class, and was able to verify her activities on the day that the pregnancy test was taken.

Questions:

1. How do you find out who is pregnant, without publicity?
2. What could be done, once the identity of the pregnant girl is confirmed? (List some alternatives.)
3. How will you deal with Jane's mother?
4. What actions will you take with Jane?

References:

Barnes, N.D., and S.E. Harrod. 1993. Teen pregnancy prevention: A rural model using school and community collaboration. *School Counselor* 41:137-140.

Dorrell, L.D. 1994. A future at risk: Children having children. *Clearing House* 67:224-227.

Harvey, S.M., and C. Spigner. 1995. Factors associated with sexual behavior among adolescents: A multivariate analysis. *Adolescence* 30:253-264.

Plotnick, R.D. 1992. The effects of attitudes on teenage premarital pregnancy and its resolution. *American Sociological Review* 57:800-811.

Suri, K.B. 1994. The problem of teenage pregnancy: An educational imperative. *Journal of Multicultural Social Work* 3:35-48.

114. TERMINATION OF PROBATIONARY TEACHER

Problem:

Lincoln School District's negotiated agreement with its teachers specifies that in the event of terminating the employment of a probationary teacher, sixty days' written notice must be given. The date this year was May 2, a Sunday.

In the high-school science department, Miss Tanner, a second-year probationary teacher, had received nothing but positive observations and evaluations from her former principal and from the science coordinator. In fact when queried in September, the principal assured the teacher that as far he was concerned, he was quite pleased with her performance and saw a long professional relationship ahead.

You took over as principal in February when the former principal became very ill. You were recently informed by the central office that next year a cut must be made in the number of sections at the 7-12 level. A choice must be made between a junior-high probationary teacher and the above-mentioned high-school teacher, both of whom were hired at the same time. Both you and the junior-high-school principal prefer to keep the junior-high-school teacher. You have been very concerned about Miss Tanner's performance as a teacher.

By the last week of April no decision had been made. On Friday of that week, a meeting was held with the superintendent, assistant superintendent for personnel, the science coordinator, the junior-high-school principal, and you. A decision was made to terminate the high-school teacher. Unfortunately this decision was not finalized until four o'clock in the afternoon and the teacher had left for the day. She must be notified prior to her return to work on Monday. The superintendent directs you to handle this situation.

Background:

Miss Tanner moved into your district two years ago from Illinois, where she was a tenured science teacher. Her recommendations from her former district were superior. She was very upset when she received a negative observation from you in March.

Questions:

1. How, at this late date, might the high-school teacher be best notified of her termination? By whom?
2. Who should normally notify a teacher of his/her termination? How?
3. How might you have avoided an "end around" once again?
4. How might you insure that this does not happen again?

References:

Nonrenewal of probationary teachers. 1993. School management advisor. Issue 25. ED372505.

Tickle, L. 1989. On probation: Preparation for professionalism. *Cambridge Journal of Education* 19:277-285.

Shreeve, W. 1993. Evaluating teacher evaluation: Who is responsible for teacher probation? *NASSP Bulletin* 7:8-19.

Vann, A.S. 1992. Preparing probationary teachers for tenure. *Principal* 71:42-44.

Youngblood, S.R. 1994. Supervising the probationary teacher: Growth and improvement. *NASSP Bulletin* 78:51-57.

115. UNCOOPERATIVE STUDENT DURING BOMB SCARE

Problem:

During your second year as a high-school principal, you ask Carl, a sophomore, to sit down in a cafetorium during a bomb scare. He refuses to comply with your directive. Suddenly he bursts out with a vulgarity and is physically escorted outside in a fireman's carry by you and six male faculty members. His parents appear the next day and accuse the school of excessive force and threaten to sue you.

Background:

Carl dresses like a member of Hell's Angels. You and he did not get along well when you were his middle-school principal. A high level of anxiety prevailed among students, faculty, and staff members during this third of a series of bomb threats on the high school.

Questions:

1. What other approaches could have been used with Carl?
2. How will you deal with Carl's parents?
3. How will the courts or attorneys view this incident?
4. If Carl's actions during the bomb threat were symptomatic of a larger problem, what steps would you take to improve his behavior?

References:

Mathers, K. 1996. Never again would we be the same: The Oklahoma City Bombing. *NASSP Bulletin* 80:38-43.

Rathbone, C.H., and R.T. Hyman. 1993. The regulation of corporal punishment: Examining the legal context in order to clarify the options for the small or rural school. ED362373.

116. WITHHOLDING GRADE OF GRADUATING SENIOR

Problem:

Joe Hernandez, a disadvantaged student, was told by his guidance counselor that he did not pass Mr. Madden's public-speaking course and therefore would not be graduating with his senior class. This student had passing third-quarter marks. No senior jeopardy letter had been sent to his parents notifying them of this situation nor did Mr. Madden notify the counselor of Joe's failure until the last minute. Joe's parents have asked for a meeting with you, the principal, to discuss this matter.

Background:

You have been principal for six months. Mr. Madden is a tenured English teacher with over twenty-five years of experience in the school district. For many years Mr. Madden has been accused of deliberately verbally abusing the economically, socially, and culturally disadvantaged students. It has been reported that guidance counselors are very careful about what students they schedule for his classes.

Questions:

1. How would you handle Mr. and Mrs. Hernandez?
2. What action would you take with Mr. Madden?
3. How will you deal with the guidance counselor?
4. How will you determine whose responsibility it was to send out the senior jeopardy letter?
5. Is there a solution to this controversial situation?
6. How will you insure that this situation does not happen again?

References:

Guide to education: Senior high school handbook. 1995. ED383444.

Larson, L., and K.K. Fine. 1991. State high school graduation and college preparation requirements compared. House Research Information Brief. ED346593.

Nathan, J. et al. 1996. Deserved, defensible diplomas: Lessons from high schools with competency-based graduation requirements. ED393214.

Reaching the goals. Goal 2: High school completion. 1993. ED363455.

117. YEARBOOK POLICIES AND STUDENT FREEDOM OF EXPRESSION

Problem:

As the high-school principal, you have just been informed by your secretary about the arrival of this year's edition of the yearbook. Recently, there has been a major problem with racial statements made by some students in a neighboring school-district yearbook. The situation was publicized in local newspapers and escalated to a level where representatives from the NAACP were called to mediate. As a result, you feel a strong need to proofread your school's yearbook before it is distributed. However, it is 11:00 a.m. and there has been a message on the morning announcements informing the students that the books will be handed out during lunch, which takes place in ten minutes. To make matters worse, the books were supposed to have arrived in time for Springfest but are two weeks late, and the students are anxious to receive their books.

Background:

This is your first year as principal, and your yearbook advisor has just completed his first edition of the yearbook. You were not aware that the book has been in the school for two days nor that students were told then the exact day and time the books would be distributed. A week before, you had met with the yearbook advisor about the situation in the neighboring school district. Your yearbook advisor reassured you that everything would be double-checked before any books were distributed.

Questions:

1. Do you allow the books to be distributed before you proofread them?

2. If you decide to proofread the book, what will you do if you find a problem?
3. What disciplinary action should you take with the yearbook advisor for not bringing you a book to review before announcing book-distribution times?
4. How could this entire situation be avoided in the future?

References:

Arnold, M.P. 1995. Student freedom of expression and high school journalism advisers: A legal and educational dilemma. ED389001.

Click, J.W. et al. 1993. Attitudes of principals and teachers toward student press freedom. *Journalism Educator* 48:59-70.

Eveslage, T.E. 1995. Stifling student expression: A lesson taught, a lesson learned. *Contemporary Education* 66:77-81.

Mencher, M. 1994. A question of censorship. *College Media Review* 33:4-7.

Oettinger, L. 1995. Censorship and the student press. ED390052.

CHAPTER SIX

Support-Staff Case Studies

Professional support staff such as psychologists, guidance counselors, reading teachers, social workers, school nurses, and librarians, among others, should provide invaluable support to classroom teachers. Their expertise and ability to focus on specific skills can enhance the instructional experiences of students at all levels of learning. Problems with these staff members may result in an interruption of necessary services to students most in need, and impact the entire staff of the school as well as the students.

Other support staff, such as school secretaries, custodians, bus drivers, and teacher aides, are also essential to the smooth operation of the schools and the district in general. The school secretaries are the first line of public relations; if they demonstrate negative or erratic behavior, then the perception of the school and the district is diminished. If the schools are dirty, cold, and unsafe because the custodians are not doing their job, then morale of the teachers and the students deteriorates and learning cannot take place. Transportation issues arise with bus drivers, which cause dangerous situations for the students and concern and fear on the part of the parents. Teacher aides perform tasks that free the teacher to spend more time with the students; when individuals in this group exhibit problem behavior, they take away important instructional time from the students. Most support staff are civil-service or union employees, which presents difficulties in removing them from their position without a long legal process. Yet these staff members frequently become a source of major concern for building principals.

Cases included in this section regarding professional support staff include a rift between the school psychologist and teachers, and concern regarding the status of a psychological referral; a problem with an excessed guidance counselor; unprofessional behavior by the reading teacher; parental concerns about a school nurse's behavior; and library problems, including an atmosphere that is not user-friendly and improving the performance of an uncooperative librarian.

Cases dealing with other support staff include a secretary with emotional problems; bus-driver alcoholism, abusive behavior, and denying transportation to a student; custodial problems, including student allegations of abuse, the "busybody" custodian, discipline of custodians for poor performance, and a custodian caught stealing money; teacher aides defying authority; a recess monitor accused of discrimination; a teacher assistant leaving her assignment to make long-distance telephone calls; and a teacher assistant undermining a teacher.

118. ABUSIVE BUS-DRIVER BEHAVIOR

Problem:

A number of students being transported to a special-education program have complained that the bus driver and aide call them names, curse, and have physically pushed them. Yesterday a fight broke out when the bus driver sprayed the bus with a disinfectant because he said the students created a foul odor.

Background:

The referrals on this particular bus have been increasing. The bus driver continually complains that the students are rude, smell, have dirty clothes, curse and show no respect.

Questions:

1. How do you find out what is really happening?
2. Who should deal with the bus driver/aides? What actions should be taken?
3. What actions will you take with the students?
4. How do you deal with negative attitudes and lack of sensitivity toward students with special needs?

References:

Barbera, M.C. 1992. Unsung heroes: Special ed. bus drivers. *Exceptional Parent* 22:24-26.

Casey, T.J. 1991. Special education transportation update and forecast. *School Business Affairs* 57:8-11.

Dorny, A., and C. Cole. 1996. Bus training handbook. ED394250.

Linder, D. 1991. Special education transportation: An eight-point tune-up. *School Business Affairs* 57:26-28.

Transporting students with disabilities: A manual for transportation supervisors. 1992. ED353727.

119. ARTS-IN-EDUCATION COMMITTEE REFUSAL TO IMPLEMENT GRANT

Problem:

Last year Mrs. Briggs, arts specialist in the Windham School District, took it upon herself to write a corporation-sponsored grant that would provide for some teachers to research dance, and then bring in a dance instructor to work with the children. The grant was awarded to her. Before any program concerning the arts can be implemented in the district, the newly formed arts-in-education committee must approve it. This committee consists of teachers, parents, and you, the principal. Over the summer the committee studied the grant and found it so vague and confusing that after two meetings no decision was made to implement the grant. Repeated attempts to have Mrs. Briggs explain exactly how this grant would work have been unproductive. Further complicating the matter was the fact that she didn't attend the second committee meeting. Since then Mrs. Briggs has gone to the superintendent to complain that the committee is "stonewalling" her grant. The superintendent has told you, the principal, to resolve the matter. You are hesitant to go back to the arts-in-education committee with the problem because the committee is totally frustrated with the matter, especially the chairman, who is a parent.

Background:

Mrs. Briggs has been a full-time arts specialist in the district for about twenty years. Over the years she has proven to be a less than competent art specialist, but for whatever reason, prior administrators have failed to terminate her. She has been bounced back and forth between the junior high and elementary schools. She is not supportive of other staff (except for a few friends on the staff consisting of other negative types), has had years of extremely high absenteeism, and the parents believe her program is a waste of their children's time and abilities. In addition, she constantly complains about almost everything to you and to the superintendent.

Questions:

1. What should you do about the grant at this time?
2. Do you think that committees like this arts-in-education committee get in the way of getting things done? How would you reunite and redirect this committee?
3. What would you do about Mrs. Briggs doing an "end run" to the superintendent?
4. Write a memo to Mrs. Briggs telling her exactly what she must do to explain the grant.

References:

Bauer, D. G. 1994. Grantseeking primer for classroom leaders. ED379762.

Bayley, L. 1995. Grant me this: How to write a winning grant proposal. *School Library Journal* 41:126-128.

Brewer, E.W. et al. 1993. Finding funding: Grantwriting for the financially challenged educator. ED364940.

Rennie, L.J., and D.F. Treagust. 1993. Factors affecting the successful implementation of whole-school curriculum innovations. ED361853.

Solomon, G. 1993. All about grants. *Electronic Learning Special Edition* 12:14-23.

120. BUS-DRIVER ALCOHOLISM

Problem:

As you enter the building this morning you notice a district school bus parked in front, and fourth-grade classes assembling in the lobby. Two parents are sitting outside your office. Ms. Sloane, a teacher, approaches and tells you, "I just saw the bus driver who is parked out front take a swig from something concealed in a brown paper bag!"

Background:

The fourth-grade classes have worked hard in the past few months to raise enough money to attend a special matinee performance at Lincoln Center. The day for the performance has finally arrived and forty-five students, two teachers, and ten parent chaperones are anxiously waiting to board the bus.

Questions:

1. How do you proceed with this bus driver?
2. What do you do with the assembled fourth-grade classes?
3. What, if anything, do you say to the parents who are still outside the office?
4. Do you cancel the trip? Why or why not?

References:

Baker, J.G. 1994. Putting drivers to the test: Transportation drug and alcohol testing. *School Business Affairs* 60:37-42.

Hammond, D., and G. Blakey. 1991. School bus drivers: Recruitment and training. *School Business Affairs* 57:26-29.

Malone, R. 1991. Safe journey. *American School Board Journal* 178:37-39.

Wright, J. 1993. Federally mandated testing of bus drivers. *School Business Affairs* 59:4-5, 8-10.

Wright, J. 1993. In your drivers' hands. *American School Board Journal* 180:34-36.

121. BUS DRIVER DEPRIVES STUDENT OF TRANSPORTATION

Problem:

Marie Hand, a student, is asked to sit down on the school bus during her transportation home from the high school. She does not comply with the driver's directive. At 4:00 p.m. you, the principal, are handed a report by the bus driver stating that the student not be allowed to ride the bus. The driver tells Marie that she should not even think about getting on the bus on the next morning's run. Parents appear the next day and accuse the school of deprivation of transportation to eligible taxpayers, and threaten to sue you.

Background:

Marie is always conservatively dressed, polite, well mannered, and courteous. You and the student get along well. According to Marie, a fellow bus rider stabbed her with a tack. A high air of anxiety prevailed among Marie, other students, and the consistently irritable bus driver.

Questions:

1. What other course of action could have been applied to the student by the driver?
2. Should you follow the driver's suggestion to terminate the child's transportation?
3. Determine the best avenue of resolution for the parents in this situation.
4. How will you deal with Marie?

References:

Ames, C. et al. 1993. Parent involvement: The relationship between school-to-home communication and parents' perceptions and beliefs. Report No. 15. ED362271.

Hill, J. 1995. Decreasing disruptive behavior among students on school buses through comprehensive school bus safety education. ED384424.

Mawdsley, R.D. 1996. Pupil transportation and the law. Second edition. NOLPE Monograph Series, No. 55. ED392128.

Neatrour, P.E. 1994. Riding by the rules: A practical approach to bus discipline. *Schools in the Middle* 4:25-27.

122. BUSYBODY CUSTODIAN

Problem:

Mr. Michael, the custodian, is taking over the building-or so he thinks. Most staff members would agree that he is not limiting his activities to those that would be included in his job description. Mr. Michael is a classic "busybody." He has his nose in everyone's business but his own, and he does not want to miss a trick! Mr. Michael, also a volunteer fireman, recently decided one morning to report to a fire, rather than to school to open up the building. He failed to notify the district before he left to fight the fire. Yet same Mr. Michael stands in the hallway and checks his wristwatch when he thinks he sees a member of the faculty coming in late to work. He also makes remarks to that faculty member about his/her "lateness." He attends every special program that is held in the building. He does his best to eavesdrop whenever staff members are involved in a discussion of student behavior problems, or parent conference results, or test results. He even lunches with the staff daily. The staff is very upset-both about the way he behaves and his comments on the way the staff does their jobs. The building is always filthy. Staff members sometimes do their own custodial work when they tire of asking Mr. Michael.

Background:

Mr. Michael is the only custodian at the Kindergarten Center, which is an "annex" (located three miles away) to the elementary school. This center was opened two years ago as a "band-aid" solution to overcrowding problems in the elementary building. Mr. Michael was hired at this time, and it was determined that one principal and one assistant principal would administer both buildings. The Kindergarten Center houses 175 students. There are six classrooms, six teachers and aides, one nurse, and one secretary in this building. The very experienced and highly motivated staff at the center have kept it running rather smoothly these past two years, but lately things seem to be falling apart.

Questions:

1. What steps must you as principal take to change Mr. Michael's behavior?
2. How will you involve the staff in this problem?
3. What role should the assistant principal play?
4. How will you deal with the custodial supervisor?

References:

Ennis, B. 1994. Custodians/security program evaluation. ED382636.

Flamm, S.R. et al. 1992. A system like no other: Fraud and misconduct by New York City School Custodians. ED352729.

Getz, R.A. 1993. Custodian quota quandary cured-Guidelines for custodial staffing. *School Business Affairs* 59:3-8.

Miller, G. 1993. Maintenance and custodial services: Getting the most for the money. *School Business Affairs* 7:18-21.

123. COACH FAILURE TO TEACH STUDENTS

Problem:

The wrestling team began practice in late November. The first match was held in early December. The athletic director attended the first home match only to see his team defeated. Mr. Champ, the part-time coach, seemed to get along well with the kids and was not disappointed by the loss. After the match the assistant coach approached the athletic director and told him that Mr. Champ had not come to any practices yet this year. The athletic director was shocked and immediately went to Mr. Champ's place of business the next morning. When asked, "Why aren't you attending practices?" Mr. Champ's response was "My job is only to coach matches; the boys must learn moves on their own." The athletic director has brought this problem to you, the principal, for assistance.

Background:

The athletic director was in desperate need of a varsity wrestling coach. The team had an assistant coach for the upcoming season who was a good administrator, but he had no knowledge of the sport or how to teach the techniques. School policy was to advertise the position in the local paper if no one within the district wanted the job. Several days later, the athletic director received a phone call from a local businessman who owned a small fitness center. As it turned out, he was a former Russian world champion in Greco-Roman wrestling and had coached wrestlers and gymnasts at the Olympic level. The athletic director set up an interview. Mr. Champ produced a coaching certificate from the USSR Fitness Ministry; a diploma with the equivalent of a master's degree in physical education from the University of Kiev; several pictures of himself coaching the Russian Olympic wrestling champion; and pictures of himself coaching an Olympic gymnastics champion. Salary was not a concern since Mr. Champ wanted to do this to be able to get to know the local students. Language was not a problem either, since he spoke broken English. Mr. Champ was hired on the spot.

Questions:

1. What are the options of the athletic director?
2. What are the consequences of each option?

3. What should the athletic director do?
4. What should you do?
5. How can you prevent a similar incident from happening in the future?

References:

Figone, A.J. 1994. Teacher-coach role conflict: Its impact on students and student athletes. *Physical Educator* 51:29-34.

Frost, J. 1995. A good coach is hard to find. *Executive Educator* 17:25-27.

Gerdy, J.R. 1995. Blow the whistle on athletic coaches. *Trusteeship* 3:22-26.

Irvine, M. 1990. One principal's approach to hiring staff for athletic programs. *NASSP Bulletin* 74:39-41.

Siegel, D., and C. Newhof. 1992. Setting the standards for coaching curriculums: What should it take to be a coach? *Journal of Physical Education, Recreation and Dance* 63:60-63.

124. CONCERNS ABOUT SCHOOL-NURSE BEHAVIOR

Problem:

Several parents have come to you, the new elementary-school principal, voicing concerns about the abrupt manner and upsetting conversations that they have had in dealing with Mrs. Atkins, the school nurse, when their children were ill. They want you to do something about her behavior as they feel that she causes anxiety in their children, who are reluctant to go to her when they are sick.

Background:

Mrs. Atkins has been at your school for six years. Other people with whom she works in the school and in the community have come to avoid her and back off rather than clash with her opinions. It is common knowledge that one local pediatrician has had very bad "run-ins" with her. Two years ago, Mrs. Atkins saved the life of a child who was choking in the cafeteria at lunchtime. In her usual direct manner, she stated to teachers and the child's parent that she had been ready, if necessary, to use a kitchen knife and perform a tracheotomy to save the student's life. She was called before the school board. They expressed their disapproval of her statements. Mrs. Atkins told the board that, since she had been trained by a local hospital, she would perform a tracheotomy if necessary, as otherwise she would be open to a malpractice suit. Since that time Mrs. Atkins has kept supplies in her office used to perform a tracheotomy.

Questions:

1. How would you respond to the parents' concerns?
2. What actions will you take with Mrs. Atkins in terms of dealing with parents and their children?
3. Is it possible to change the behavior of an experienced, mature, opinionated teacher or staff member?
4. Whom else will you consult concerning this controversial nurse?

References:

Fryer, G.E., Jr., and J.B. Igoe. 1996. Functions of school nurses and health assistants in U.S. school health programs. *Journal of School Health* 66:55-58.

Harrison, B.S et al. 1995. The impact of legislation and litigation on the role of the school nurse. *Nursing Outlook* 43:57-61.

Mehl, R.A. 1990. The school nurse: Beyond the band-aids. *Principal* 70:22-23.

Role of school nurse. 1991. ED346682.

125. CUSTODIAN STEALING MONEY

Problem:

Mr. Considine noticed a continuous depletion of change that had been left in his classroom drawer and discussed this problem with a colleague, Mr. Evans. The teachers decided to set up a hidden camera in Mr. Considine's classroom overnight, since the money always disappeared between the time he left school and before he returned at seven the following day.

The second evening, the night custodian, Mr. Hoover, entered Mr. Considine's room and did his job. On the way out of the room he stopped and listened for any sounds coming from the hallway. Hearing nothing, he opened Mr. Considine's desk drawer and took out some change. He put the money into his pocket and left the classroom for the night. The next morning, Mr. Considine discovered the change missing. The entire incident had been captured on videotape.

Within a few days this tape became common knowledge throughout the school. The story spread quickly, since other faculty members had noticed similar discrepancies and had suspicions of their own regarding Mr. Hoover. The head custodian, Mr. Bronson, learned of the tape today and has come to you, the principal, demanding action. He wants you to call the two teachers into your office immediately and reprimand them for their devious and reprehensible behavior.

Background:

Mr. Hoover lives in the community and has worked at the school for nine years. He has been reprimanded several times for drinking on the job. Other complaints have been made about him, including suspicions of theft, but there has never before been any hard evidence against him.

Questions:

1. Can the tape be legally used against Mr. Hoover in bringing charges against him?
2. What actions will you take with Mr. Hoover?
3. How will you deal with the teachers?
4. How will you keep this incident contained within the building so that it does not escalate into a major public-relations problem?
5. How will you handle the "demand" of the head custodian as well as his supervision of his staff?

References:

Chatman, E.A. 1990. Alienation theory: Application of a conceptual framework to a study of information among janitors. *RQ* 29:355-368.
Ennis, B. 1994. Custodians/security program evaluation. ED382636.

126. DIFFICULTIES WITH REASSIGNED P.E. TEACHER

Problem:

You are the new principal at LaSalle Elementary School. A group of parents have come to you about Mr. Hamilton, the physical-education teacher recently reassigned to your school. They are very concerned about his teaching practices and his dealings with their children, and are demanding that he be replaced.

Background:

Mr. Hamilton has been tenured for eighteen years, and is two years away from retirement. He was an ineffective high-school teacher for many years. He had trouble communicating with high-school students, lost control of his classes when doing certain activities, taught while sitting down on a set of bleachers, did not maintain accurate student records for grading purposes, and fell asleep in class on numerous occasions. Early last year while touring the school with a group of parents, the high–school principal found Mr. Hamilton asleep in his class. Later in the year Mr. Hamilton fell asleep during one class period and his students left the class before the end of the period. When he woke up and found his class absent, Mr. Hamilton marked the entire class truant.

Three years ago, when Mr. Hamilton began to have major problems with his students and administrators, the school district tried to excess him by stating that he was the least senior teacher in his certification area. He felt that the administration was discriminating against him, and went to the union and the NAACP. After Mr. Hamilton won his case, he was transferred to your school. You have just found out that Mr. Hamilton has health problems, including high blood pressure and diabetes, and is moonlighting six nights a week to support his family.

Questions:

1. Identify the major issues in this case study.
2. How can you find out if Mr. Hamilton's lack of energy is a physical problem or one caused by his working a second job?
3. How would you deal with Mr. Hamilton? Since he is two years away from retirement, are there any win-win options you might pursue?
4. How would you handle the parents' concerns?
5. With whom else should you consult regarding Mr. Hamilton's behavior?

References:

Brar, H.S. 1991. Unequal opportunities: The recruitment, selection and promotion prospects for black teachers. *Evaluation and Research in Education* 5:35-47.

Fejgin, N. et al. 1995. Work environment and burnout of physical education teachers. *Journal of Teaching in Physical Education* 15:64-78.

Foster, M. 1990. The politics of race: Through the eyes of African-American teachers. *Journal of Education* 172:123-141.

Mars, H. et al. 1995. Novice and expert physical education teachers: Maybe they think and decide differently, but do they behave differently? *Journal of Teaching in Physical Education* 14:340-347.

O'Sullivan, M., and B. Dyson. 1994. Rules, routines, and expectations of 11 high school physical education teachers. *Journal of Teaching in Physical Education* 13:361-374.

127. DISCIPLINE OF CUSTODIANS FOR POOR PERFORMANCE

Problem:

School custodians at the Eastern School have not been cleaning the classrooms, vacuuming the rugs, or cleaning the bathrooms. This has been a problem for the past two years, but the situation has worsened in recent months.

Background:

The school custodians have been approached on several occasions by classroom teachers and by you, the principal, regarding the unsanitary and unsightly appearance of the classrooms. The head custodian, Mr. Banks, has informed the teachers that the vacuum is broken and that district maintenance has not repaired it. Apparently, it has been broken for three months. You and the teachers feel that the custodial staff is involved in the "passing-the-buck" syndrome.

Questions:

1. What procedures can be set up to insure that the classrooms and bathrooms are cleaned properly?
2. Who is directly responsible for supervising custodial staff when the building and grounds supervisor is not on site?
3. How can we train custodians to clean properly in order to create a sanitary learning environment?
4. Is the staffing level of the custodial staff appropriate?

References:

Chatman, E.A. 1990. Alienation theory: Application of a conceptual framework to a study of information among janitors. *RQ* 29:355-368.

Holayter, M.C. 1990. With awards and recognition, our custodians really clean up. *Executive Educator* 12:13.

Montgomery, A. 1994. Caring is not enough: Assessing community in high schools. ED382755.

128. EXCESSED GUIDANCE COUNSELOR

Problem:

Ms. Swanson is an elementary-school counselor and serves as chairman of the Committee on Special Education. As of March, it became known that her position was being excessed in favor of a school psychologist, a decision made administratively in order to satisfy state Committee on Special Education mandates. At that point, Ms. Swanson explored options to continue her employment in the district. She considered bumping the 60 percent high-school guidance position, as she had seniority in this area. She requested the opportunity to do an administrative internship in the remaining 40 percent of her time. However, the superintendent denied this request. Unable to continue working at only 60 percent salary, Ms. Swanson ended her employment as of June 18. On June 21, pertinent records were discovered to be either missing, misplaced, or stolen.

Background:

Ms. Swanson had worked her first year under the former principal and was generally considered competent and successful. Eighty percent of her job was doing counseling with students and working in classrooms. Her second year coincided with a change in principals and a change in Committee on Special Education guidelines. You, the newly appointed principal, placed the entire CSE responsibility with her. She regularly spent many evenings working quite late to finish paperwork. As the year progressed, her attitude became more and more cynical. After the end of the school year Ms. Swanson's whereabouts were unknown.

Questions:

1. What should you do upon discovering that certain CSE records are missing?
2. How could this situation have been avoided and what safeguards will you develop to prevent similar instances in the future?
3. How will you deal with the rumors currently circulating among the faculty about the disappearance of the records and Ms. Swanson?

References:

Boley, E. 1994. Restructuring: School counselors can make a difference. ED367920.
Godbold, L.H. 1994. Middle school guidance counselors: Are there enough? ED374385.

129. IMPROVING PERFORMANCE OF UNCOOPERATIVE LIBRARIAN

Problem:

Ms. Daniels is a high-school librarian. Occasionally her library is used for administrative meetings and small district workshops. Teachers have commented among themselves that the library is often unavailable for their students to use. Teachers are discouraged by the librarian from bringing in classes for research or for cooperative instruction with the librarian. Ms. Daniels says she is busy with ordering, maintaining the library collection, and with scheduled district meetings that cause the library to be closed to students. The staff is not informed of the arrival of new books and media that they have requested for the curriculum. Materials remain packed in boxes for months waiting to be made available.

Recently, the library was closed while it was painted and carpeted. Everyone anticipated that it would be approximately one month before the library would be ready to open. You, the principal, provided additional custodial and aide time to assist Ms. Daniels. Each day Ms. Daniels came to school in her finest clothes, manicured nails, and immaculately groomed, and was unprepared to do any work. She spent a great deal of time drinking coffee and socializing in the back room while the custodians and aides tried to figure out what to do. You saw what was happening and spoke to Ms. Daniels but she made no attempt to change. The library opened two months later than anticipated.

Background:

Ms. Daniels is a tenured school librarian with twenty years of experience in a large urban school system with a strong teachers' union. She has been assigned to various schools at both elementary and secondary levels because of school closings, reopenings, and changing enrollment patterns. Her changes in assignment have been voluntary as she has district seniority among 16 librarians and has first choice of positions that become available.

Her reputation among teachers and principals is poor. She does very little work with the students. The teachers complain that their students are poorly prepared in library skills. Since becoming tenured, Ms. Daniels has received satisfactory evaluations from various principals before you, despite her poor reputation.

Questions:

1. Outline a step-by-step action plan for dealing with Ms. Daniels.
2. What recommendations would you make to her to assist her in improving her performance?
3. Whom would you enlist to assist you in this matter?

References:

Moe, L. 1994. Partnering: Teachers and library media specialists. *Ohio Media Spectrum* 46:10-13.

Pearson, R.C. 1989. A critical relationship: Rural and small school principals and librarians. ED390589.

Schon, I. et al. 1991. The role of the school library media specialists. *School Library Media Quarterly* 19:228-233.

Stronge, J.H., and V.M. Helm. 1992. A performance evaluation system for professional support personnel. *Educational Evaluation and Policy Analysis* 14:175-180.

Sutton, D. 1995. So you're going to run a library: A library management primer. ED385282.

130. RECESS MONITOR ACCUSED OF DISCRIMINATION

Problem:

Mrs. Best, a mother of a fifth-grade student, has just come into the office complaining that recess monitors are exercising prejudice in their disciplinary dealings and decisions. One playground monitor reported to you, the principal, that she had witnessed at close range a student hitting another student in the side of the face. The monitor stated that the student accused of hitting was disrespectful and not responsive when told to go into the building. He was given one day of recess detention. Mrs. Best expressed concern that her son felt he had not been treated fairly; that the other student had pushed him, and therefore also deserved recess detention. Mrs. Best accused the monitor of not telling the truth, and accused both you and the monitor of having separate sets of standards for different ethnic groups. The monitor and the boy who was hit in the face are white. The student who moved in on the other student and then hit him is black.

Background:

The monitor has been employed by the district for several years and has two children in attendance at the elementary school where she works. She has been observed to be highly conscientious in her duties and insightful in her dealings with children. Because of these traits she has also been asked to fill in as a substitute for special-education teaching assistants when they are absent. This is the first time any such incident has occurred with the monitor.

Questions:

1. How do you determine what actually happened?
2. How will you deal with Mrs. Best?
3. What actions will you take with the students who were involved in this situation?
4. What will you say to the playground monitor?

References:

Jambor, T. 1994. School recess and social development. Dimensions off Early Childhood 23:17-20.

Kraft, R.E. 1989. Children at play—behavior of children at recess. *Journal of Physical Education, Recreation and Dance* 60:21-24.

Pellegrini, A.D. 1995. School recess and playground behavior: Educational and developmental roles. ED379095.

Pellegrini, A.D. et al. 1995. The effects of recess timing on children's playground and classroom behaviors. *American Educational Research Journal* 32:845-864.

Pellegrini, A.D., and P.K. Smith. 1993. School recess: Implications for education and development. *Review of Educational Research* 63:51-67.

131. RESTRUCTURING THE LIBRARY INTO A USER-FRIENDLY RESOURCE

Problem:

This is your first year as principal of the Woodlands Middle School. Many teachers have complained about Ms. Johnson, the media and library specialist. Teachers are quite upset that the library is an inadequate source of information. The books and other resource materials in the library are basically an embarrassment. The library lacks a user-friendly atmosphere and students and teachers do not want to go there. The librarian does not encourage or help the students. This problem has existed for at least five years and continues to upset the teachers.

Background:

Two years ago, Ms. Johnson made an improvement effort when she issued an anonymous questionnaire to the teachers. Since that questionnaire two years ago, there has been no improvement. Recently teachers were upset when they found out that as a study-hall teacher, Ms. Johnson sent fifteen students to the library during one period. This was in direct conflict with the policy established by Ms. Johnson herself years ago that no more than five students in study hall could be sent to the library during any one period.

Questions:

1. How do you handle teacher anger over this most recent problem?
2. How do you deal with Ms. Johnson?

3. How do you help restructure the library into a user-friendly resource?
4. How do you rebuild teacher confidence in Ms. Johnson if she does a turnaround and makes improvements?

References:

Baron, D.D. 1996. Recent dissertation research and the individual school library media specialist. *School Library Media Activities Monthly* 12:49-50.

Stronge, J.H., and V.M. Helm. 1991. Evaluating professional support personnel in education. ED331150.

Wilson, L. 1991. Teaching librarians to teach: A course in library use instruction. ED341389.

Young, E.M. et al. 1995. Evaluating school library and media specialists: From performance expectations to appraisal conference. *Journal of Personnel Evaluation in Education* 9:171-189.

Yucht, A.H. 1992. The elementary school librarian's desk reference: Library skills and management guide. Professional growth series. ED377849.

132. RIFT BETWEEN SCHOOL PSYCHOLOGIST AND TEACHERS

Problem:

Dr. Peters was hired at Mason Elementary School two years ago. He is not a team player when it comes to working with the teachers. The teachers have come to you, the new principal, and told you that many of them have been placed in embarrassing positions because of his actions. The first– and second-grade teachers state that they will not refer any more children to him. Last week, in front of one of them, Dr. Peters told a parent that the teacher did not know how to properly teach the parent's son.

Background:

Although he is in his forties, this is Dr. Peters' first experience in an educational setting. He is unaware of the school curriculum and often tells parents the complete opposite of what they have been told by the other teachers involved in the situation. Furthermore, he often gives parents the wrong information or downgrades the classroom teacher to them. Dr. Peters doesn't eat in the teacher's room nor does he associate with teachers in any way. On a professional basis he does not listen to or respect the opinions of the classroom, resource-room, or reading teachers.

Questions:

1. How do you counsel Dr. Peters regarding his inappropriate and unprofessional behavior?
2. What actions would you take if Dr. Peters does not respond to your direction to be more of a team player?
3. How do you resolve the problems he has created with parents by giving them incorrect information and talking negatively about the classroom teachers?
4. What team-building activities would you conduct to try and close the rift that has been created between the teachers and Dr. Peters?

References:

Kramer, J.J., and S. Epps. 1991. Expanding professional opportunities and improving the quality of training: A look toward the next generation of school psychologists. *School Psychology Review* 20:452-461.

Mucha, L. 1994. A survey of teacher perceptions of school psychologists as consultants: A factor analytic study of evaluation in the consultation process. ED377412.

Reschly, D.J., and L.M. Connolly. 1990. Comparisons of school psychologists in the city and country: Is there a "rural" school psychology? *School Psychology Review* 19:534-549.

Rosenfield, S., and D. Nelson. 1995. The school psychologist's role in school assessment. ERIC Digest. ED391985.

Sandoval, J. 1993. Personality and burnout among school psychologists. *Psychology in the Schools* 30:321-326.

133. SECRETARY WITH EMOTIONAL PROBLEMS

Problem:

For the past four years, Ms. Martin's life has been in a constant state of crisis. Her problems are real and they are serious. Whenever she is in the midst of a crisis (which lasts for a few days) she can be found crying and telling her story to anyone who is available. Several times during the day she asks someone, "Did you hear what happened to me?"

Ms. Martin is one of only two secretaries in a large school, and there is much work to be done. When she is upset, she is unable to perform her duties. She is frequently away from her desk being consoled or if she is at her desk, she is telling her story to whoever is available. Staff members are beginning to complain that she is not pulling her weight; faculty members are beginning to complain that they are being held hostage as she tells her story.

When these situations arise she is encouraged by you, the principal, to go home. Rather than do this she nobly musters up her strength and says, "No, but thank you. I think I can make it." Moments later, however, she is asking someone "Did you hear what happened to me?"

Background:

Ms. Martin is a secretary in a small school district where she also resides. Many of the teachers and staff are from town and know each other both professionally and personally. Ms. Martin has been a secretary in the school for seven years.

Questions:

1. For how long should sensitivity and compassion be shown to Ms. Martin when she is clearly in a state of distress?
2. Should she be forced to go home when she's in crisis?
3. What referral services should be consulted regarding her situation?
4. How will you prevent Ms. Martin's behavior from upsetting the students and the teachers?

References:

Banach, W.J., and J.A. Kasprzyk. 1989. What secretaries say about principals. *Principal* 68:42-43.

Casanova, U. 1991. Elementary school secretaries: The women in the principal's office. ED336835.

Portraying a positive image: A guide of effective public relations for educational office personnel. 1989. ED325964.

Pounder, D.G. et al. 1995. Leadership as an organization-wide phenomenon: Its impact on school performance. *Educational Administration Quarterly* 31:564-588.

134. STUDENT ALLEGATION AGAINST CUSTODIAN

Problem:

You have just received calls from two frantic mothers whose fourth-grade daughters did not get off the school bus. As you finish the second call, a teacher brings the two crying girls into your office. They tell you that Mr. Harney, the custodian, locked them in a custodian's closet. When Mr. Harney is called in and confronted with the girl's allegation, he admits that he did lock them in the closet because "they took my broom."

Background:

Mr. Harney has been a custodian in the building for ten years. During this time he had also been a part-time bus driver. Mr. Harney (the father of two elementary school students in a neighboring district) has been spoken to on several prior occasions for "kidding and playing with" the students while he was working. He allows them to do such things as joke with him and take and hide his cleaning utensils.

Questions:

1. What course of action will you pursue with Mr. Harney? Describe both short-term and long-term plans.
2. With whom will you consult regarding this matter?
3. How will you respond to the parents?
4. How will you deal with the girls?

References:

Anderson, K.M., and O. Durant. 1991. Training managers of classified personnel. *Journal of Staff Development* 12:56-59.
McBride, P.G. et al. 1992. Creating custodial classes: An instructional program guide for custodial workers. ED353378.

135. TEACHER AIDES DEFY AUTHORITY

Problem:

There are two aides in the special-education department of the high school who assist classroom teachers. They are not always where they are supposed to be and don't follow through on assignments. Teachers have made complaints regarding these aides working with students, helping them too much, or not showing up at all. They have had excessive absences, arrive to class late, and disrupt the teacher by starting personal conversations. The instructional personnel have to use their valuable time to correct these situations.

Background:

The two aides are local community members. They have not attended any conferences or classes to enrich their special-education abilities. They each have a high-school diploma. Last year the aides were spoken to individually regarding their absences and told to attend conferences or take classes.

Questions:

1. What actions should you, as principal, take to correct this situation?
2. What would you include in your performance improvement plan for the aides?
3. What role will the teachers play in this plan?
4. How can you follow an aide's schedule on a daily basis?
5. How can you create a positive attitude towards these aides on the part of the teachers?

References:

Achilles, C.M. 1993. The teacher aide puzzle: Student achievement issues: An exploratory study. ED363956.

Holmes, R.M. 1991. A lesson learned: Teacher's aide or child's aide. *Intervention in School and Clinic* 26:159-162.

Martella, R.C. et al. 1995. Teaching instructional aides and peer tutors to decrease problem behaviors in the classroom. *Teaching Exceptional Children* 27:53-56.

Palma, G.M. 1994. Toward a positive and effective teacher and paraprofessional relationship. *Rural Special Education Quarterly* 13:46-48.

Pickett, A.L. et al. 1993. Promoting effective communications with para-educators. Ed357586.

136. TEACHER ASSISTANT ACCUSED OF UNDERMINING TEACHER

Problem:

Mr. Marks is a new teacher on your staff. He has a master's degree, many years of teaching experience, and a sincere interest in becoming a permanent member of the community and your school staff. His references were excellent. He seems to be a stable person in his thirties who is very "into" a career in education. You immediately like what you see going on in his classroom. Mr. Marks has good organizational skills and quickly established a rapport with students. His lessons are creative, well planned, and appropriate for his students. You sense you have hired a quality teacher and wish to keep him by giving him good teacher assistants and much support.

Midway through the year, Mr. Marks comes to you to tell you he is being undermined by the teacher assistant, Mrs. Green. He describes covert acts of negativism and outright defiance on her part. He says he has been hesitant to come to you because he thought he could handle it alone and because he knows the assistant is highly respected by other staff. He agrees that her abilities are excellent. However, he states that Mrs. Green is subtly and cleverly negating what he does by undermining his authority and presenting mixed messages to the students. He is beside himself with frustration and anger. His attempts at handling the problem have ended with denial, angry outbursts, and a rally of support by other faculty members for the assistant. He wants her out of his room.

Background:

Mrs. Green has a degree in psychology and certification in elementary education. She is working on a master's degree in special education. On several occasions, she has assumed the role of a teacher to cover for a staff member who was ill, left a position, or was on leave. She is dependable, bright, creative, energetic, and very cooperative with persons she admires and with whom she agrees. You also know she has a temper and can be difficult.

Questions:

1. How can you determine what is really happening between Mr. Marks and Mrs. Green?
2. What steps would you take to help promote a positive working relationship between this teacher and his assistant?
3. What difficulties may occur when assistants are allowed to perform additional responsibilities (such as covering for a teacher on leave) that are outside of their job requirements?
4. What can you do to insure positive working relationships between teachers and teacher assistants?

References:

Feinman, J.M. 1991. Teaching assistants. Journal of Legal Education 41:269-288.

Lamont, I.L., and J.L. Hill. 1991. Roles and responsibilities of paraprofessionals in the regular elementary classroom. B.C. Journal of Special Education 15:1-24.

Lawler-Prince, D., and J.R. Slate. 1995. Administrators', teachers', and teaching assistants' self-evaluation of pre-school programs. ED392167.

Pickett, A.L., ed. 1988. Paraprofessional bibliography: Training materials and resources for paraprofessionals working in programs for people with disabilities. ED302045.

Wadsworth, D. E., and D. Knight. 1996. Paraprofessionals: The bridge to successful full inclusion. Intervention in School and Clinic 31:166-171.

137. TEACHER ASSISTANT LEAVING ASSIGNMENT TO USE TELEPHONE

Problem:

Ms. Lorenzo is a second-year teacher assistant. Over the past four months, she has been leaving the classroom daily to make phone calls. During the past month, four long-distance calls to a South American country were made on the school phones; these calls cost over seventy-five dolars. When confronted about the calls, Ms. Lorenzo denies that she made them. She states that she has only made local calls. She storms out of the room, screaming that the school will regret blaming her for these calls.

Background:

Ms. Lorenzo has just planned a trip to the South American country to which these calls were made. Ms. Lorenzo has also left class an average of three times a day to make calls to unknown places.

Questions:

1. What should you do when an employee leaves his/her assignment several times a day to make personal phone calls?
2. How can you determine who made these phone calls to the South American country?
3. What action should you take with Ms. Lorenzo?
4. What can you do to insure that no other calls are made to foreign countries or out-of-state on the school phone?

References:

Educational assistants: Suggested personnel policy guidelines for school districts. 1990. ED325972.

Paraprofessional training manual. 1990. ED334151.

Pickett, A.L. 1990. Paraprofessionals in education: Personnel practices that influence their performance, training needs, and retention. ED337329.

The role of the paraprofessionals in Utah schools: The selection: preparation, and utilization of paraprofessionals in education. 1990. ED340684.

Strachan, P. 1990. A training program for paraprofessionals: Classroom management skills. ED325233.

138. TEACHER WITH PERSONAL AND PROFESSIONAL PROBLEMS

Problem:

Mr. Dean, an elementary-school art teacher, has been chronically late. He comes strolling into the school thirty minutes after the scheduled report time. During the first marking period, he turned in grades for a class he did not have. He rarely attended the faculty meetings. His appearance became haggard. It was rumored that he sometimes slept in his car or in the school. He was scheduled with a back-to-back prep and lunch period and often left school during that time to have a few drinks. Last semester, you reprimanded him for buying a beer at lunchtime and placing it in the refrigerator in the physical-education office. Mr. Dean also cannot get his official transcript released because he owes a balance on the college's bill for his final semester.

When talking with Mr. Dean, you, the principal, find that his stories often differ from one telling to the next. He is skillful in changing subjects and circumventing issues. One of the fourth-grade students complained to you that she did not feel comfortable with the way Mr. Dean hugged her. On the plus side, Mr. Dean is very personable and is well liked by the students. Although he is disorganized with his plans, his lessons are considered good. The students are much more excited about the art program since he has been the teacher.

Background:

Mr. Dean was hired last year, due to the retirement of the art teacher. He arrived with ten years of private-school European teaching experience and a newly completed master of fine arts degree. He was the choice of the outgoing art teacher and the principal at that time. His first half-year went rather routinely. There seemed to be a renewed energy coming from the art room. Mr. Dean decided to rent/share a small house with the son of one of the secretaries, since his wife and two small children live in another state. However, he moved out after two months and did not pay any rent. This situation climaxed with a sheriff's deputy arriving at school to serve Mr. Dean with a summons to appear in court. He resolved this matter by filing for bankruptcy. You were hired as the new principal this year and must decide if Mr. Dean should be rehired next year.

Questions:

1. Mr. Dean has many problems. List these in order of priority, from the most critical to the least critical.
2. What data do you need to help you decide if Mr. Dean should be rehired next year? How will you obtain that information?
3. Develop an assistance plan that you could implement with Mr. Dean.
4. With whom should you consult regarding this problem?

References:

Ernst, K. 1996. Art in your curriculum. Our open-door policy. *Teaching PreK-8* 27:26, 28.

Gates, J.T. 1995. Arts teacher education reform: Recruiting a new profession. *Teacher Arts Education Policy Review* 96:34-39.

Likes, D. 1995. How art teachers can work with non-arts administrators. *Art Education* 48:23-24.

Mawdsley, R.D. 1992. Sexual misconduct by school employees. NASSP Legal Memorandum. ED350671.

Susi, F.D. 1995. Student behavior in art classrooms: The dynamics of discipline. Teacher Resource Series. ED386412.

139. UNPROFESSIONAL BEHAVIOR OF READING SPECIALIST

Problem:

The entire staff has had it with Mrs. Brooks, the reading specialist. They feel that you, the new middle-school principal, should do something other than ignore the situation. Mrs. Brooks is constantly late for work. She comes in at 8:45 a.m. while the rest of the staff must arrive by 8:30 a.m. She is late for her classes—anywhere from ten to fifteen minutes. She does not handle her own discipline problems. Rather she sends them back to class. She has a "language arts" class every afternoon–on paper only. She was given two weeks to set up the standardized-test answer booklets and her classes were canceled. Many mistakes were made in completing this task. On the day of the first test there was total chaos. During the entire testing period, she did nothing. She brought in coffee and doughnuts and was seen by faculty members reading the newspaper while she was overseeing the tests. After the testing period, she took another two weeks to erase the stray marks on the test booklets.

Background:

Mrs. Brooks is tenured and has been a reading teacher for eleven years. During that time she has worked in four different elementary schools. During her assignment in the last school, she worked so poorly with the staff that she alienated herself to the extent that she transferred out of the building. Last year the principal who was about to retire gave her an unsatisfactory evaluation. She was so enraged that she had her husband, who is a lawyer, challenge this evaluation by threatening a lawsuit against the principal. The principal backed down and revised Mrs. Brooks' evaluation.

Questions:

1. You are now Mrs. Brooks' principal. What is your plan of action?
2. List the specific problems outlined in the case study.
3. What directives will you give Mrs. Brooks?
4. How will you deal with the concerns of the entire staff?

References:

Cheng, Y.C. 1996. Relation between teachers' professionalism and job attitudes, educational outcomes and organizational factors. *Journal of Educational Research* 89:163-171.

Fang, Z. 1996. A review of research on teacher beliefs and practices. *Educational Research* 38:47-65.

Pearson, L.C. 1995. The prediction of teacher autonomy from a set of work-related and attitudinal variables. *Journal of Research and Development in Education* 28:79-85.

140. UNPROFESSIONAL BEHAVIOR OF SCHOOL PSYCHOLOGIST

Problem:

Ms. Wilson is a psychologist who has been in the district for three years. She is highly opinionated and feels that her skills, as a Ph.D. in clinical psychology, are better than those of many of her colleagues having school-based training.

Ms. Wilson has had difficulty in relating to the staff. She has antagonized people by disputing their decisions at inappropriate times. For example, in retesting a special-education student, she walked into his classroom and stated in front of the students that he was emotionally disturbed, not learning disabled, and did not belong in the room. The district's Committee on Special Education later upheld the current classification. In another instance, at a parent/staff meeting, she told the director of a school for severely handicapped children that a child she was testing was autistic and not mentally retarded, and therefore was inappropriately placed. An outside evaluation upheld the current placement.

Ms. Wilson is a hard worker and believes strongly in staff development. She has spearheaded several in-service workshops and has worked closely with the director of pupil personnel services.

Background:

Ms. Wilson is one of 15 psychologists in a large suburban school district. A teacher-in-charge who is not an administrator chairs the department. The director of pupil personnel services coordinates all special area programs and is the administrator responsible for approximately 75 staff members.

The teacher-in-charge has worked closely with Ms. Wilson. He rejected a number of her reports and helped her rewrite them. He assigned a peer mentor to work with her on district procedures and expectations. At the end of her first two years, the teacher-in-charge recommended against rehiring her. When she was being considered for tenure, he made a recommendation against it. The director of pupil personnel services, who recommended her for tenure, supervised her. Tenure was recently granted by the board of education.

Questions:

1. How can Ms. Wilson be helped to develop more appropriate skills for her job?
2. As a building administrator, what can you do to develop staff relations between the psychologist and the rest of the staff?
3. As a director of pupil personnel services, what would you do?

References:

Christenson, S.L. 1995. Families and schools: What is the role of the school psychologist? *School Psychology Quarterly* 10:118-132.

Holdzkom, D. 1995. Designing a personnel management system for school psychologists. *Journal of Personnel Evaluation in Education* 9:159-170.

Murray, B.A. 1996. The principal and the school psychologist: Partners for students. *NASSP Bulletin* 80:95-99.

Stronge, J.H. et al. 1994. How do you evaluate everyone who isn't a teacher? An adaptable evaluation model for professional support personnel. ED387537.

Williams, K.J. et al. 1990. The relation between performance feedback and job attitudes among school psychologists. *School Psychology Review* 19:550-563.

Index (Numbers refer to case number not page number)

SOURCE BOOKS ON EDUCATION

REFORMING TEACHER
EDUCATION
Issues and New Directions
edited by Joseph A. Braun, Jr.

CRITICAL ISSUES IN FOREIGN
LANGUAGE INSTRUCTION
edited by Ellen S. Silber

THE EDUCATION OF WOMEN
IN THE UNITED STATES
*A Guide to Theory, Teaching,
and Research*
by Averil Evans McClelland

MATERIALS AND STRATEGIES
FOR THE EDUCATION OF
TRAINABLE MENTALLY
RETARDED LEARNERS
by James P. White

TEACHING THINKING SKILLS
Theory and Practice
by Joyce N. French
and Carol Rhoder

TELECOMMUNICATIONS
A Handbook for Educators
by Reza Azarmsa

SECONDARY SCHOOLS
AND COOPERATIVE LEARNING
Theories, Models, and Strategies
edited by Jon E. Pederson
and Annette D. Digby

TEACHING SCIENCE
TO CHILDREN
Second Edition
by Mary D. Iatridis with a
contribution by Miriam Maracek

KITS, GAMES AND
MANIPULATIVES FOR
THE ELEMENTARY SCHOOL
CLASSROOM
A Source Book
by Andrea Hoffman
and Ann Glannon

PARENTS AND SCHOOLS
A Source Book
by Angela Carrasquillo
and Clement B. G. London

PROJECT HEAD START
*Models and Strategies for the
Twenty-First Century*
by Valora Washington
and Ura Jean Oyemade Bailey

EARLY INTERVENTION
*Cross-Cultural Experiences
with a Mediational Approach*
by Pnina S. Klein

EDUCATING YOUNG
ADOLESCENTS
Life in the Middle
edited by Michael J. Wavering

INSTRUMENTATION
IN EDUCATION
An Anthology
by Lloyd Bishop
and Paula E. Lester

TEACHING ENGLISH
AS A SECOND LANGUAGE
A Resource Guide
by Angela L. Carrasquillo

THE FOREIGN LANGUAGE
CLASSROOM
Bridging Theory and Practice
edited by Margaret A. Haggstrom,
Leslie Z. Morgan,
and Joseph A. Wieczorek

READING AND LEARNING
DISABILITIES
Research and Practice
by Joyce N. French,
Nancy J. Ellsworth,
and Marie Z. Amoruso

MULTICULTURAL EDUCATION
A Source Book
by Patricia G. Ramsey,
Edwina B. Vold,
and Leslie R. Williams

RELIGIOUS HIGHER EDUCATION
IN THE UNITED STATES
A Source Book
edited by Thomas C. Hunt
and James C. Carper

TEACHERS AND MENTORS
*Profiles of Distinguished
Twentieth-Century Professors
of Education*
edited by Craig Kridel,
Robert V. Bullough, Jr.,
and Paul Shaker

MULTICULTURALISM IN
ACADEME
A Source Book
by Libby V. Morris
and Sammy Parker

AT-RISK YOUTH
Theory, Practice, Reform
by Robert F. Kronick

RELIGION AND SCHOOLING
IN CONTEMPORARY AMERICA
*Confronting Our
Cultural Pluralism*
edited by Thomas C. Hunt
and James C. Carper

K–12 CASE STUDIES
FOR SCHOOL ADMINISTRATORS
Problems, Issues, and Resources
by Marcia M. Norton
and Paula E. Lester